To Dance with the Devil's Daughter

TO DANCE WITH THE DEVIL'S DAUGHTER

God's Restoration of the Rev. Grady Caldwell

BILL LIGHTLE

GRADY CALDWELL

Mill City Press, Inc.
212 3rd Avenue North, Suite 290
Minneapolis, MN 55401
612.455.2294
www.millcitypublishing.com

ISBN-13: 978-1-62652-136-0
LCCN: 2013938436

Cover Design by Alan Pranke
Typeset by Steve Porter

Printed in the United States of America

ALSO BY BILL LIGHTLE

Made or Broken: Football & Survival in the Georgia Woods

Mill Daddy: The Life & Times of Roy Davis

My Mother's Dream: Baseball with the Bankers

For Kathleen Jones Caldwell

and the late Leola Caldwell –

women of love, devotion, and faith

FOREWORD

The story of Grady Lee Caldwell, Jr. is revealed with remarkable candor in this inspiring book. From a young boy growing up in Albany, Georgia, during the Civil Rights Movement of the 1960s, to remarkable leadership as the first African American football player at Albany High School, and one of only three in the state of Georgia, Grady's story will touch your heart.

This bright young man with a promising future ahead of him succumbed to the temptations of sin that brought him down to the pit of despair. Then, through the continued faithfulness and prayers of his wife, Kathleen, and his devoted mother, and many family members and friends, Grady came home to the Lord, leaving the wilderness behind to become a servant of Jesus Christ.

As I read Grady's story, I thanked the Lord for His redeeming grace, and at the same time gave thanks for Kathleen whose faithfulness blessed my heart. A verse of Scripture kept coming to mind, Romans 5:20, "For where sin abound, God's grace does much more abound."

When you see what God did for Grady Caldwell, you will never again wonder if God could somehow use you.

Dr. J. Robert White
Executive Director
Georgia Baptist Convention

INTRODUCTION

God's grace is absolutely amazing! It is amazing how He knew what it would take to break me of myself and place me in a position that I was willing to do His will, and not my own. I always believed in God but had never really had the need to call on Him for myself until I realized I was addicted to drugs and I could not stop on my own. I had to go from a place of promise, to the problem of addiction and all of its negative consequences including prison, before totally committing myself to His purpose for me – pastoring.

I used to ask God, "Why don't You just take away my addiction and I will do Your will. I know You can. You are sovereign. I know some people You have done it for." His answer for me was not what I wanted to hear. He said, "I will not just take away your addiction for two reasons: First, you would think that you did it yourself; and secondly, you would never spend the time in My Word that I need you to do in order to accomplish My purpose for you."

But God didn't just leave me in a state of desperation. He gave me a covenant promise through His Son and my Savior Jesus Christ in John 8:31, "...If you abide in My Word, you are My disciple indeed. And you shall know the truth, and the truth shall make you free." Jesus, The Truth, has made me free today!

In Luke 10, Jesus spoke a parable about the Good Samaritan. There was a man going from "Jerusalem to Jericho and fell among thieves." Well, I was that man who fell among thieves. But now through God's amazing grace and His mercy I am that Good Samaritan looking for others who have fallen "among thieves" and letting them know that if God could redeem and restore me, He can do the same for them. But it must be done His way. God is not going to allow some of us to be mediocre Christians.

To whom much is given much is required.

Pastor Grady Caldwell
New Mercy Baptist Church
Griffin, Georgia
December 2012

PREFACE

When Grady Lee Caldwell, Jr. began smoking the highly addictive and sometimes deadly concoction of freebased cocaine, it was with his friend Robert E. Hines, a minister and teacher in Albany, Georgia. Rev. Hines soon became deranged because of drugs and once covered the picture of Jesus Christ on his Bible with his own picture. After that, Grady severed his relationship with the wayward minister. The sickness was too much for him. Rev. Hines later turned violent and was sent to prison for life in 1984 for killing his girlfriend's brother. The years following the killing, Grady was dying a different kind of death. It would be the first time in his life he called on God to help him.

By the early 1980s, Grady had become director of alumni affairs at Albany State College. He had a promising career in academia or anything else he chose. People respected him, and he had a way of making others like him. He had easily made friends all his life, captivating people by both his charm and intellect, and was well liked among his colleagues on campus. He would also become a drug addict living some days with suicidal behavior.

Grady was married to Kathleen Jones whom he had dated since they were students at Albany High School. They were both among the first group of African Americans to integrate and graduate, Grady in 1967 and Kathleen the following year, from that once all-white school. It had been a time of turmoil and epic change. It had been a time of racial violence. Grady became the first African American to play on the Albany High football team by the mid-1960s. On that team and at that school, he overcame racial threats and humiliation. Once, a dead rattlesnake was placed in his locker in efforts to force him off the team and out of that school. He refused to leave neither.

Grady had come of age during the 1950s and '60s when African Americans were beaten and killed throughout the South by some whites full of hatred and unwilling to accept the end of their segregated culture. He had seen the fiery hatred of the Ku Klux Klan up close. He had survived those troubled times. During his boyhood, he was mentored by civil rights leaders and spent time with Dr. Martin Luther King, Jr., when he stayed in Albany.

In the early 1970s, with so much promise and before his fall, Grady ran for the Albany City Commission. Even though he was defeated, he later became part of a successful federal lawsuit that changed voting from at-large to individual wards in Albany's local elections. This led to African Americans being elected to the Commission for the first time in the city's history. He continued to make civil rights history. People who knew him were not surprised. Some predicted he would accomplish much in the years ahead. They would all have to wait.

By the time Grady began freebasing cocaine with Rev. Hines, he was facing the greatest danger of his life: Himself. His drug addiction led to shoplifting, financial hardship for his family, and a lifestyle outside of marriage in which he traded cocaine for sex. Sometimes the sex was with two or three women at a time in a cheap and dirty Albany motel room while his wife was at home taking care of their children, trying to hold the family together, and praying hard for her husband's recovery and for him to become the man she had married. Grady was in hell. In some ways he put those who loved him there, too. He repeatedly went to jail for shoplifting and forgery. He asked God to help him all this time, but the drugs and his life of crime did not stop. Then he went to prison.

ONE

From inside the house the young boy looked out the back window and saw gray smoke rising high into the night sky. He was not scared, but others in that house were. There was good reason to be scared. The smoke came from a field behind the house at 914 Cedar Avenue in Albany, Georgia, where a large wooden cross was set ablaze by men behind the sheets of the Ku Klux Klan, the white supremacist organization. Their faces were not visible, but their hatred was. These were terrorists.

Dr. Martin Luther King, Jr. was in that house with that young boy, Grady Caldwell, Jr., who was about 12 at the time. It was the early 1960s when Grady saw the flaming cross from the home of Dr. William Anderson, president of the Albany Movement, and an osteopath. He and other African American leaders in Albany had begun organizing and leading mass protests in efforts to attack segregation over a broad front. The face of white resistance was found among the couple of hundred Klansmen near Anderson's house that night who had set the cross on fire and with a bullhorn announced over and over, *"Get those niggers! Get those niggers! Get those niggers!"*

King came to Albany at the behest of the Anderson family who had asked the nationally-recognized civil rights leader, born in Atlanta, to help in efforts to end Albany's strict code of racial segregation. He had come more than once during the early 1960s, and when he did, he stayed at Anderson's home. Grady spent a lot of time there with his friend Gil, Anderson's son. That night when fear and hatred were so visible, so close, Dr. King and Anderson noticed the two boys looking out the back window at the Klan rally. Grady's attitude toward the rally was that it was something to be watched, much like a circus sideshow, not something of which to be afraid. Dr. King and Anderson knew better. They quickly ushered the two boys away from the window and to an inner room in the house. They knew the Klan was capable of bombings, lynching, and other acts of terrorism. The boys may not have known it, but the men did.

All night long there was tension in the house. Prayers were said by those inside. If Grady did not know then the extent the Klan would go to prevent African Americans from having the same rights as whites, he would soon learn as he came of age during the 1960s. That particular night, with the burning cross and the hateful announcements from the bullhorn, there would be no physical violence. The Klan rally ended without incident. The racial troubles and fear among African Americans in Albany would continue.

"I don't remember being scared that night. I was probably more excited. I do remember the white sheets and the burning cross," Grady said. "He (Dr. King) was just another man to me that night. He had no significance then. That would come later. We knew that night we had those men to protect us. Later I realized how dangerous it really was."

Gil Anderson was the same age as Grady, and they had been friends since they were in the second grade together. Days before the burning cross and Klan rally, bricks had been thrown through the Anderson's window, one almost hitting Gil and his sister. After that, the front windows had been boarded up for protection against other potential acts of violence. With plywood covering the windows, it looked as if the Anderson's family home had been abandoned. He said the night with his friend, Grady, and Dr. King, when the Klan rallied outside of his home had been "one of the scariest times of my life." It could've been worse.

"Some of our neighbors had shotguns and told my father they would use them against the Klan if they had to. They were ready for war that night," Gil said.

• • •

An African American physician, Dr. William Reese, delivered Grady Lee Caldwell, Jr. into this world on July 21, 1949, at his home at 807 Corn Avenue. It was the same neighborhood he would come of age in, where his friend Gil lived, and where the Klan once threatened him. Reese's wife, Mamie, had been dean of women at Albany State College. She was also Grady's godmother. Early on and later with death sometimes so close to him, strong and loving women would both guide and help save Grady's life.

Grady's mother Leola Caldwell was born in 1909 in Tift County, Georgia, about 40 miles east of Albany. She would live to be a 100. Leola's mother, Rosa Hailey, could not read or write but had four daughters, and all would graduate from college. Rosa married three times, having outlived each husband. Leola's maiden name was Hodges. Education was stressed hard in that family, and so it would be when Leola herself became a mother. Rosa was a strong and determined woman who was a mid-wife and delivered several hundred babies in Tift County, family members said. Leola earned a vocal scholarship to a boarding school, Boggs Academy, for African American students near Waynesboro, Georgia. She later attended Paine College in Augusta and graduated

3

from Albany State College with an education degree. She would teach school for about 40 years.

Leola taught at African American schools in Albany, including Madison Street Elementary, and she made extra money working as a hair dresser. She once owned some rental property. Before Grady was born, she and Grady Caldwell, Sr. had one other child, Loretta, born in 1943. Grady found strength and direction from Leola when he was young, and later, as a man on a path of self-destruction, it would be her strength again he would need. His father would have little impact on guiding Grady's life. In 1951, Grady Caldwell, Sr. died of an ulcerated stomach. His death never should have happened that way, Loretta said.

"Daddy died at Phoebe, and he was in such severe pain. He was just strapped into a chair," Loretta Caldwell Travers said. "He wasn't treated because the white doctors refused to help him. There were no black doctors available when he needed them." Phoebe Putney Hospital was founded in Albany in the early 1900s, and it treated African Americans in segregated facilities. When African American doctors were unavailable, other African Americans often went without medical treatment.

Loretta's memories of her father were fond ones. She said the reason her mother never remarried was because, "The Caldwell men were strong. Nobody could fill their shoes."

Loretta graduated from Monroe High School in Albany at 16 and earned a piano music scholarship to Virginia State University. She went on to study for three years in New York City at the Juilliard School of Music, which was and is known throughout the world for its excellence in teaching musicians. She received an undergraduate degree from Clark-Atlanta University and master's degree from Illinois State University, both in music education. By 2011, she had retired after teaching music in public schools for about 40 years. By then she was in charge of the music program for St. Patrick's Episcopal Church in Albany.

"I loved my father because of his personality. He was more outgoing. She was very reserved," Loretta said. "He was the one with an outgoing personality and everybody loved him. Grady became like that. Everybody liked him, too."

Grady Caldwell, Sr.'s family was from Albany, and he worked at the family-owned Caldwell Cleaners on the corner of Corn Avenue and Madison Street, not far from his home. During World War II, he served in the Army in Europe defending his country, but his death reflected one of the many ways in which African Americans were victimized by longstanding racism, his family said. It would be left up to Leola, whose nickname was "Momma Lee," to guide her children through this challenging and dangerous period. They would need discipline and education. She would do her best.

"Momma Lee wanted them to have the finer things in life. She put Grady and Loretta in an organization called Jack & Jill of America," Kathleen Caldwell said. "It was primarily for preachers' and teachers' kids. It exposed them to the arts, music, and they took field trips."

Leola did more than that for her two children. She enrolled both of them in the Hazard Laboratory School on the Albany State College campus just east of the Flint River. Hazard's rigorous academic setting and strict discipline was designed to prepare African American children for successful lives while stressing the value of a formal education. Grady attended kindergarten there, grades one through three he was at Madison Street Elementary where is mother taught, and fourth through seventh grades back at Hazard. At Hazard, much was expected from students in terms of discipline and academic work, Grady said.

Tuition was free and some of the students were selected from a poor neighborhood off Washington Street near railroad tracks, Kathleen said. Classes were limited to around 20 students. Teachers were well trained, dedicated, and some even inspiring. If a student misbehaved, corporal punishment was used by the teacher to correct the behavior. There were few discipline problems. These students were expected to behave, study, and achieve. Their parents, like Grady's and Kathleen's, were the foundations of such expectations.

"Back then the Hazard School was created to show what education could do for black students. We had great teachers," Kathleen said. "They were committed. The discipline is one of the things I remember. Mostly, we were well behaved. It was expected."

In the fifth grade, Grady was taught by Mrs. Mary Clark. She taught all the academic subjects and had each student open a savings account at First State Bank. She told her students about the importance of tithing to their churches, Grady said. Mrs. Clark chose Grady and his friend, Gil, to take the money she collected from her students and walk to the First State Bank, not far from their school, and have the money deposited in their individual accounts. When Kathleen was in the fifth grade, Mrs. Clark selected her as one of the students to deposit money in bank accounts.

"She helped develop our self-confidence. We would do plays and in one I played Patrick Henry. 'As for me, give me liberty or give me death,'" Grady said. He was quoting Henry from Virginia, one of the leaders during the American Revolution.

Another Hazard teacher was Ms. Beatrice Moultrie-Benson who Kathleen said was an excellent grammarian teaching proper English in both speaking and writing. She controlled her classroom; the students did not. "She would smile when she strapped you for misbehaving," Kathleen said.

Hazard was providing a strong educational beginning for Grady and instilling in him a view that he was not "inferior" to whites, he said. The view among Albany whites that they were superior to African Americans began with the founding of the city by the mid-1830s when cotton planters brought in African slaves to do the crushing work. When slavery ended in 1865, it was eventually replaced in Albany and the South by Jim Crow laws, a brutal system of segregation. It was a two-tier world where whites through laws, customs, and hatred stripped from African Americans their political rights that were afforded them through the U. S. Constitution. This was the world Grady and other African Americans inherited by the 1940s and '50s. Success in formal education is one way to challenge the view of white superiority. Leaders at Hazard School knew this. Hazard was preparing Grady for what was to come.

Gil was drawn to Grady early and "looked up to him" but "felt sorry for him" because his father had died. As their friendship grew, Grady often turned to Gil's father for guidance. The two boys were close until the Anderson family moved from Albany to Michigan in 1964, Gil said. Gil attended Morehouse College in Atlanta, graduated from the Michigan State Medical School in 1975, and began practicing medicine. By 2011 he was still in the profession working as an obstetrician and gynecologist outside of Flint, Michigan. He remembers Grady as a boy he always wanted to be around.

"It was just a natural attraction for the two of us. We were both good students, we enjoyed school, and we lived in the same neighborhood," Gil said. "We were both put in positions of leadership and responsibility as kids. Grady always had a level of maturity that seemed to be beyond his years. And he was fearless."

That fearlessness would manifest itself in many ways throughout Grady's life. There was a big dog in Gil and Grady's neighborhood, and it was usually chained by its owner. When the two boys walked by the dog, it barked menacingly at them. It always scared Gil. One day when Grady wasn't with Gil, the dog was off the chain and chased Gil. He ran as fast as he could to get away from the dog. He later told Grady what had happened.

"Grady told me, 'Don't be afraid of that dog. He won't bother you if you don't act scared.' Then Grady had me walk with him to the dog's yard," Gil said. "I didn't really want to go but I did. I followed Grady."

Grady had a switchblade knife with a pearl handle that he carried in his pants pocket. On the way to the dog, Grady pulled his knife out of his pocket. When the two boys arrived where the dog lived, they noticed he was not chained. Gil was scared. Grady showed no signs of that emotion. He opened his knife and held it in his right hand. The dog rushed them barking loud and threateningly, like it always did, Gil said.

"When the dog came toward us, Grady said, 'Stand still and don't be afraid. He won't bother us.' And we stood there and we didn't move. I thought the dog was going to tear us up," Gil said. "But he ran up to us and just barked. In a few seconds later, he walked away, just like Grady said he would."

With his mother and his teachers pushing Grady in one way, there were times when he was being pulled toward another. Grady's house on Corn Avenue was near two public housing projects, Holly Homes and Washington Homes. In front of Grady's home was Carver Park where African Americans, who were denied access to public facilities such as the Tift Park pool and public libraries, had their own swimming pool and a small library. Carver Park included ball fields and basketball courts that Grady played on. Grady learned how to swim there and became a lifeguard. He became such a good swimmer that the Red Cross asked him, and he accepted, to go to Tifton, Georgia, to teach other African Americans to become lifeguards for an African American pool. From his house he once saw something else at Carver Park.

He was about ten or 11 when he saw a large group of boys gathering at Carver Park. They weren't there to play basketball or football. None of the boys carried the look of sportsmanship on their faces. These were two rival gangs. One was from Holly Homes and the other from Washington Homes. Grady saw the fight between about "20 boys on each side" in one of the fields at the park. He saw it all.

"This was serious stuff. No one had guns. At least I don't remember any," Grady said. "But they had knives, and I saw boys get cut. It was not uncommon for someone to get beaten for going into another neighborhood." Lines were drawn by these gangs based on what housing project they lived in, Grady said. When the lines were crossed, there'd be trouble. Grady was being drawn into all of this. By the time Grady had left Hazard School and was in the eighth grade at Carver Junior High, Leola was worried about what direction in life he was going to take. He was beginning to spend time with some of the toughs, some of those from the street gangs of the housing projects. Leola wanted something else for her son, something better. She continued to stress a life of education, achievement, and cultural refinement. Grady did well in school. His grades were better than average. Which direction would he take? "I wanted to be on both sides of the street. I lived a block away from the housing project," Grady said. "That's where my friends were."

Around the time he saw the gang fight at Carver Park, his mother had arranged for Grady to take piano lessons. With each lesson, she gave Grady money to pay his teacher. Grady was to ride his bike to the instructor's house, receive the lessons, and pay his teacher. At least that's what his mother believed. Grady took a few lessons only, but after that used the money to buy candy, soft drinks, and other things. This went on for some time. Then at one point Leola learned the truth when she spoke with the teacher to see how Grady was progressing on the piano. That ended her efforts to have Grady play the piano. "Momma wanted me to be cultured. But at one point when I was young, I thought all the men I knew who played the piano were sissies," Grady said.

Grady may have been torn between both sides of the street, but he didn't get into any trouble with the law nor was his behavior ever rude or disruptive at school. During his eighth-grade year, some of his teachers were impressed by his classroom efforts. One of those teachers was Walter Judge, who taught Grady pre-algebra at Carver Junior High. Judge would spend about 40 years in education, earning a Ph.D. at Florida State University and eventually serving as associate superintendent of Dougherty County Schools. Judge said Grady was "a very inquisitive student who didn't just want to know the answers to word problems, he wanted to know why."

At one point during that school year, Judge took Grady to his ninth-grade class and had him complete some pre-algebra problems to impress on them that they, too, could achieve. Judge said he never had problems with Grady in terms of discipline, and he had always been respectful to teachers and classmates having "been taught discipline at home." Grady turned in his work on time, worked hard, and was one of Judge's top students. Judge predicted then the young boy would accomplish many good things, just like his mother had hoped for. "I just knew he would have a bright future. He had everything a young man could want. He was bright," Judge said. "His mother was caring and supportive and gave him anything within her means. I just knew he'd go far."

About the time Judge was beginning to recognize promise in Grady's academic work, some days he carried a switchblade knife to school. He didn't do it to hurt anybody or because he was threatened by other students. He was "never suspected of doing anything wrong because he was a teacher's son," Kathleen said.

"I did it just to prove something to the boys from the projects. I wanted to fit in. I didn't want to appear to be smart," Grady said. "I remember at Carver in class sometimes giving the wrong answer even though I knew the right one. I just didn't want to appear to be the class brain."

One of the boys from Holly Homes housing project who became friends with Grady was Robert Thomas, Jr., known as "Bob-Bob." He got his nickname from his sister Janice because when she was young and tried to say "Bobby" it came out Bob-Bob. Grady and Robert played sandlot football and basketball together at Carver Park, became close friends at

Carver Junior High School, and remained that way through high school. They did a lot together, but they never got into any serious trouble.

"We never got in any trouble. I had parents who leaned on me. They kept me straight," Robert said. "Grady was smart in school and fun to be around. We didn't cause any problems. We just had fun together in our neighborhood."

Robert Thomas, Sr. was considered a "pioneer" in the Albany Movement and owned the Harlem Barbershop, around the corner from Dr. William Anderson's office on South Jackson Street. Dr. Anderson's office was where local civil rights leaders often met. Thomas attended those meetings with Anderson and other leaders and helped plan marches and church rallies during the movement. He was arrested during these marches and demonstrations. Along with his wife Wynona, he provided needed discipline while stressing the importance of an education to their son and two daughters. Robert Thomas, Jr. would not disappoint his father.

Grady, Robert, Ernest Jenkins, Gil, Larry McCartherens, and other boys often played basketball at a home next to the Andersons' on Cedar Avenue. It was behind Gil's house where the Ku Klux Klan had burned crosses when Dr. Martin Luther King, Jr. was inside. That group of boys "were together all the time" playing sports, having fun and coming of age in a time of great social and racial change, and in a time of danger and violence, Grady said. Grady, Larry, and Gil had met a man in Gil's neighborhood who had served in the Air Force. He befriended the boys, giving them model airplanes that they spent hours putting together.

Fatherless after the age of two, Grady found something more in the Anderson household than friendship with Gil and the opportunity to meet someone who would become one of the world's most recognized citizens – Dr. King. Gil's father, Dr. William Anderson, offered Grady a model and instructions about living a decent life and challenging injustice in Albany. Anderson became Grady's surrogate father. "Grady was always responsive to the direction I'd give him," Anderson said.

While providing guidance to Grady and his own son, Anderson said he tried to shield both of them from the pains and fears of segregation and racism in Albany. It was a difficult task. "What I distinctively remember was that when we rode with Dr. Anderson, we'd ride down alleys," Grady said. "We never went the same route twice. It was only when I got older I realized how dangerous it was."

Until he was in high school, Grady had had little contact with whites in Albany. Once while shopping downtown with his mother, he mistakenly pulled on the dress of a white woman believing it was his mother. Leola Caldwell quickly intervened on her son's behalf. "I remember the fear on my mother's face when that happened," Grady said. "I just didn't understand things then."

In September 1962, the *U.S. News & World Report* published a story on the ongoing racial unrest in Albany. At that time, whites outnumbered blacks about 36,000 to 20,000, according to the story. Whites controlled the local industries while two large federal payrolls, Turner Air Force Base and the Marine Corps Supply Center, were feeding the local economy. The same federal government was being petitioned by local blacks to end racial segregation in public facilities. Lawsuits had been filed requesting the U.S. government to desegregate bus lines and depots, libraries, parks, playgrounds, swimming pools, theaters, the municipal auditorium, recreation centers for teenagers, toilet facilities, and schools. The story went on to report:

> Before the Negro campaign began last year, Albany was considered a rather moderate Southern city. There had been a minimum of racial trouble. A Negro once held elective office of coroner. There has been little activity by the Ku Klux Klan or White Citizens Council – even during the recent racial disturbances. The climate of race relations began to heat up early in 1961, when Negroes stepped up their demands for desegregation.

C. B. King, a local African American attorney for The Albany Movement, was once beaten bloody with a cane being swung by Dougherty County Sheriff Cull Campbell. King had gone to the jail to see clients. After the attack, Campbell said, "Yeah, I knocked the hell out of that son-of-a-bitch, and I'll do it again. I wanted to let him know...I'm a white man and he's a damn nigger."

During this same violent and troubled period, *Newsweek* magazine reporters interviewed Albany Police Chief Laurie Pritchett. "There are three things I like to do," Pritchett said. "Drink buttermilk, put niggers in jail, and kick reporters' asses."

This was the world in which Grady Lee Caldwell, Jr. was coming of age.

As a boy, Grady would attend the same church, Mt. Zion, where Dr. King preached during the movement and where mass rallies were held. The church was on Whitney Avenue. Today it's part of the Albany Civil Rights Institute. Grady attended regularly with his mother and sister,

Loretta. He attended Sunday school classes taught by Ozell Kelly, and in that church he "accepted Christ as my Savior at an early age," Grady said. He sang in the choir and was remembered by others as having a beautiful voice. He grew up with faith in God.

TWO

A couple of blocks from where Grady was born on Corn Avenue, Kathleen Jones was born at 509 West Gordon Avenue. It was August 31, 1950, about a year after Grady was born. Her home had three bedrooms, and there were eight other children born to Joseph Jones, Sr. and his wife, Lois. Kathleen or 'Kat' had three sisters and five brothers. She knew of Grady when she was a little girl. She became fond of him in junior high and fell in love with him by high school. She would remain that way about him even decades later when his drug addiction almost killed him and sent him to prison. They first kissed on the front porch of that house on West Gordon Avenue. Nearly 50 years later, they both remembered it. Grady described it as *"WOW!"*

Kathleen's family had one of the few telephones in the neighborhood and often neighbors came to use it or borrow a cup of sugar from Lois. She always welcomed other children into their home, Kathleen said. She has "good memories" about coming of age in that neighborhood during the 1950s and into the '60s. There was a strong feeling of love and community among the families living along her street and on others nearby. Her family provided love, support, and discipline. Like Grady's upbringing, there was a strong emphasis on earning a college degree and becoming successful. Her parents were providing the proper foundation. There was fun along the way.

On Saturday mornings while her parents slept late, Kathleen and some of her brothers and sisters would walk to a neighborhood grocery store owned by Mr. Gus Washington. There they would buy hard candy and cookies. But they didn't have any money. Their parents had a monthly account with Mr. Gus, and he allowed the children to charge what they wanted. At the end of the month, when it was time to pay the bill, Joseph and Lois Jones were sometimes surprised and then remembered they had slept late on the weekends–and remembered they had nine children.

"We knew they'd be a little angry but it wouldn't last too long. I just remember those Saturday mornings as being something we always looked forward to. Going down to Mr. Gus's for candy," Kathleen said.

Kathleen's father had served in the military, worked as a custodian at the post office, and painted houses to make extra money. He had had a previous marriage before marrying Lois. She was 16 when they married; Joseph was 26. Lois was in high school and tried to keep the marriage a secret from school administrators, concerned that if they found out, they would no longer allow her to attend. She had been selected as valedictorian at Madison High School in Albany. Sometime before the graduation ceremony, the principal learned about Lois's marriage and rescinded the honor as valedictorian. Lois would graduate, attend college for a period but not earn a degree. She encouraged her children to attend college and six of the nine would earn degrees, including Kathleen.

Lois possessed striking physical beauty. Her mother, Kathleen's grandmother, had been "part Cherokee Indian and her father was half white," Kathleen said. That beauty was inherited by Kathleen and her sisters. Kathleen's maternal grandmother was "disowned by her family" after she became pregnant outside of marriage. For Lois, there'd be other challenges inside her marriage.

"Daddy was a real jealous man because of Momma's beauty. My momma made him think he was king, but she was running the show," Kat said.

With Lois running the show at home with "the heart of a servant," Joseph was running a different kind of show outside of his house and away from his family, Kathleen said. Like the kings of old, he was living a philandering life for years with several local girlfriends, and this was shared with Kathleen and her sisters after "they became of age as young ladies." It was more than just flirting, and it was well known to Lois. Kathleen's father was a fashionable dresser and he shopped for clothes at Rosenberg's, a downtown clothing store offering the latest in styles to local customers. He wore fine clothes, drank fine liquor and "it was unknown to us but he partied with his girlfriends on the weekends at American Legion Post 512," Kathleen said of her father, who died in 1967. Joseph Jones, Sr. took care of his family financially. His children and wife were well provided for. He lived another life during the weekends. Like his marriage to Lois when she was still a high school student, his secret life didn't stay that way long.

"Me and my brothers and sisters didn't know for quite a while. But Momma knew," Kathleen said. "When I found out about it, I accepted it. I just thought it was something that happened. Momma told me and my sisters that when we look for husbands and get married, they'll have girlfriends, too."

He had his girlfriends but Kathleen's father remained jealous of other men if they looked too long and too interested at his wife.

Lois worked outside of the home after her children began attending school. She became the first African American truant officer for the Dougherty County Schools. At one point she worked in a reading lab under Dr. Walter Judge, Grady's junior high school teacher. Lois sent her children to the Hazard Laboratory School on the Albany State campus, where Grady attended, giving them academic rigor and discipline. Kathleen took dance lessons at her mother's behest. The foundation was being laid, one of discipline, effort, and accomplishment. Lois was providing that for Kathleen as did Leola for Grady.

By Grady's ninth-grade year, he was attending Southside Junior High with Kathleen a grade behind him at Carver Junior High. Grady was captain of the football team, well liked, and making good grades, just like what was expected from him. One of his best friends, Ernest Jenkins, found Kathleen pretty, very pretty. A lot of boys did too. Ernest knew that Grady and Kathleen knew one another, sometimes spent time together, more friends than sweethearts at that point. Ernest asked Grady if he would talk to Kathleen on his behalf. He wanted to know if Kathleen would be interested in spending time with him, maybe, eventually, becoming his girlfriend. Grady thought about what Ernest had wanted him to do. He thought about how pretty Kathleen was and how much he liked being around her, talking with her, taking walks with her through Carver Community Center. Every time Grady was around her, he liked the feeling he got inside. Grady thought about what Ernest wanted, but he thought more about what he wanted. He wanted more time with Kathleen himself. The message from Ernest never got to Kathleen.

"Grady never told me about what Ernest had said. I knew Ernest. He was a good guy," Kathleen said. "But I liked being with Grady. I guess it was about then that we started spending more time together. Not really dating. Not yet."

By the fall of 1964, Grady was enrolled as a tenth-grader at Monroe, by then the only high school in Albany for African Americans. The following year Kathleen would be a student there.

During this same period Kathleen's family moved into a home they bought at 1017 Whitney Avenue, a few blocks west of the house they had been renting on West Gordon Avenue. They were the first African American family to live on that particular block of Whitney Avenue. The change did not come without resistance. After the first few days they had been in their new home, car riders at night and sometimes during the day threw trash and empty drink bottles into their yard. One of their white neighbors moved out not long after Kathleen and her family moved in their new home. Then one night something else happened.

Kathleen's sister, Beverly, was a student at Albany State College, studying sociology and secondary education, and one night she had a date and returned home around eleven. She was about to enter the front door of her new home when she saw something and began to scream. It was a rattlesnake. Thick and long it lay on her front porch next to the door. She ran from the front porch to the back of the house. She was still screaming. Her family inside heard her and thought something terrible was happening to Beverly.

"We heard her scream and opened the front door and saw a huge rattlesnake. But it was dead," Kat said.

The family called the police who came to their house, heard their story and took away the dead snake. The family never learned who had left the snake on their front porch. When the police left that night,

Kathleen learned something about her mother she had not known before they found the dead rattlesnake. Lois and her father kept a gun in the house. It was a .22 caliber pistol. Lois got the gun and sat in a chair the rest of the night looking out a front window. She was going to protect her family. That kind of protection worried her children.

"I remember screaming and running that night. I was so scared," Beverly said. "I was hysterical. Momma got her gun and sat at the window all night."

"My mother said it was a pretty big snake and whoever put it on our porch would come back to get it," Kathleen said. "Momma said, 'I'm going to sit here and I'll shoot them when they come back.' "

Lois Jones didn't shoot anyone that night. No one came back looking for the dead snake, Beverly said. Kathleen and Beverly tried to convince their mother to put her gun away and go to bed. Instead, she stayed at the window all night until morning came.

"At one point a car did slow down in front of our house and Momma flicked the blinds back and forth," Kathleen said. "Then the car took off. We were all scared."

Lois had taught her children since they were young to be resolute, to stand for fairness and decency for all people, and to stand for your own personal dignity. It began in little ways. Even during a Saturday trip for an ice cream cone. The Arctic Bear, a popular restaurant that served hamburgers, milkshakes, and ice cream cones, stood on the corner of Slappey Boulevard and Oglethorpe Drive when Kathleen and Beverly were growing up. Whites were served in the front of the restaurant, but African Americans were supposed to place their orders at a window in the back of the restaurant. It was the way of the South. It was the way of Albany.

On one particular trip to the Arctic Bear, Lois told her children to defy the segregated ways of the city and place their orders in front of the restaurant along with white customers. The children did as they were instructed, but an employee refused to take their orders. They were told to go to the back window with other African American patrons. The children did not go to the back of the restaurant but returned to tell their mother.

"Momma said, *'Demand that you be served!'* So we tried again in front and they still said no. Then we went back and told Momma," Beverly said. "We were going back and forth and back and forth and finally we gave them our orders in the back. But then Momma told us to get in the car and we left. We didn't get any ice cream that day."

Lois was "passionate" about standing against Albany's strict racial and dehumanizing desegregation, and this encouraged Beverly, born in 1947, to join the local civil rights marches in 1961 and '62. She attended mass meetings, sang in churches, heard Dr. King speak, and, like hundreds of others, she would be arrested by the Albany police.

"I heard Dr. King speak two or three times. And I shook his hand. It was just wonderful to hear him," Beverly said. "Even today I can remember exactly what it was like to look into his eyes. He was so passionate."

The Saturday before Easter in1962, Beverly was protest marching with a group that ended their walk at city hall where they knelt on their knees to pray. Albany police moved in, arresting many of the marchers, including 15-year-old Beverly. "That day I was arrested I refused to stand up when the police put their hands on me," Beverly said. "I just wouldn't get up. They drug me on my knees and I was bleeding."

She was taken to the Albany jail, but later that night she and some of the other marchers who were arrested, were transported to the Camilla jail about 25 miles south of Albany. She was kept there four nights, and her parents were not notified of her whereabouts. Beverly and the others arrested in Albany were not physically abused in Camilla. Jailers brought protesters one meal a day of grits, fried fatback, a slice of bread and a cup of water. The marchers sang freedom songs and prayed while their families in Albany worried about them, wondering where they were and if they'd ever see them again. After the fourth night in Camilla, Beverly and others were transported back to Albany and released. Her mother cried and hugged her hard when she saw Beverly was unhurt and home again. The family rejoiced. The movement continued.

"Dr. King told us to march with dignity and keep our eyes straight ahead," Beverly said. "We held hands when we marched. And always looked straight ahead...We always looked straight ahead."

Beverly graduated from Albany State in 1969, taught school for a short period in Wilkinson County, Georgia, in the central part of the state. She later lived in both New York City and Washington, D. C. She has worked as a social worker for the Head Start federal program that provides educational help for poor children. In 1974 she married Al Walden from Virginia. They met in New York. In 2011 the couple was living in Douglasville, Georgia.

Not long after the marches ended in Albany in the early 1960s, Beverly's sister, Kathleen, and her boyfriend Grady would ultimately accept a challenge that required the kind of determination that Beverly displayed while marching and being arrested. Beverly had watched the two over the years as their affection and love for one another was growing. She had been involved in the movement that would change Albany, the South, and the country itself, making it a better place to be. Grady and Kathleen would make their contributions by the mid-1960s.

"Kathleen and Grady by then were sweethearts and young lovers," Beverly said. "*WOW!* What can you say? They were always together."

THREE

By the fall of 1964, when Grady was a sophomore at Monroe High, he went out for the football team but didn't stay long. During one practice session, the coach used a thick wooden paddle to repeatedly whack players on their butts because he had become disgruntled with their efforts. He didn't get Grady. Refusing to accept that kind of mean-spirited discipline, Grady quit the team.

"I played in the band for the rest of the year. I had been a good football player in junior high and I did want to play," Grady said. "As it turned out, I would play but not at Monroe."

Grady completed the tenth-grade at Monroe, kept his grades above average, and decided to transfer to Albany High School where a small number of African Americans had enrolled a year earlier to join the senior class. Grady would be one of 31 African Americans who transferred into Albany High in the fall of 1965. All of them were juniors. That group would be the first students of color to spend two years at Albany High. All 31 would graduate in 1967. The school had been built in the 1950s on Residence Avenue, it had been segregated until 1964, and by the time Grady arrived, it served approximately 1,500 students. There were no African Americans on any of the school's athletic teams. Grady Caldwell was about to change all of that.

By mid-August 1965, Grady and his boyhood friend, Ernest Jenkins, the one who wanted Kathleen to be *his* girlfriend, became the first two African American players to join the Albany High football team and attend its infamous, hellish two-week pre-season camp called Graves Springs. The camp was located a few miles outside of Albany in Lee County on the Muckalee Creek. There players since the 1930s had trained, practicing three times a day in a 100 degrees, with no water breaks during their two-hour plus practice sessions. I attended that camp in the early 1970s. It was a physical killer. Hazing had been common, so were deadly water moccasins in and around the cinder block barracks. Coaches worked the players unmercifully. One Albany sports writer from the 1960s said it was Graves Springs where players were "made or broken." In 2004 I published a book, *Made or Broken: Football & Survival in the Georgia Woods*, about how for decades coaches took their players to Graves Springs, into the swamplands and away from their families, to forge a team. Grady and Ernest would face another kind of challenge.

After the first day of practices, Ernest left the camp and the team, unwilling to take any more racial slurs and physical threats from some white players who sought to keep their team as segregated as the world they had come of age in. Ernest walked out of the camp, hitched a ride on a garbage truck, and returned to Albany. He never returned to the camp or the team. Grady was now the lone African American player among about 60 white teammates and an all-white coaching staff. He was in the woods where much violence had been aimed at African Americans for decades by the Klan. Grady knew this by that point in his life. He was no longer the young boy who had seen the flaming crosses of the Klan but didn't fully understand the danger it represented. From 1880 to1930, the Cotton Belt of Southwest Georgia had 196 documented lynchings of African Americans. From 1961 to 1965, the year Grady went to Graves Springs, 21 civil rights murders were recorded in the Deep South. Grady may not have known these deadly numbers, but he knew full well the dangers of his era, of his South. He was determined to stay at Graves Springs.

"I wanted the challenge. I didn't think of it then as part of the civil rights movement or how it played into Albany's history at that time," Grady said. "I just wanted to prove I could do it, and Albany High had a good football team back then."

Grady was about five feet seven and weighed only about 130 pounds. He was small but tough. He had to be. Primarily he would play defensive back and occasionally the coaches at camp worked him at running back. During scrimmages at Graves Springs when Grady worked with the offense and carried the football, from his teammates who tackled him, he sometimes heard this: *"Nigger, we're gonna kill ya! We're gonna kill ya!"*

Grady's girlfriend, Kathleen, didn't want him to go to Graves Springs, fearing what might happen to him there. She was a sophomore at Monroe and old enough to understand racial hatred. She was in love with Grady. She worried about his safety at Graves Springs and prayed that God would watch over him. Leola, Grady's mother, didn't try to stop her only son from joining the all-white team and attending Graves Springs, but she worried for her son's safety like Kathleen did. His uncle, Ira Bryant of Tifton, tried to convince Grady not to go to Graves Springs where whites could physically hurt him or worse. He knew the dangers that confronted African Americans during that period. Grady went to Graves Springs anyway.

At camp he learned that not everyone was against him. Head Coach Harold Dean Cook had a deserved reputation of being a tough, tough disciplinarian. He had winning teams and was respected by his players and townsfolk alike. He immediately became concerned for Grady's safety. At night, instead of Grady sleeping next to his white teammates, Cook had Grady sleep next to him and the other coaches.

Cook's family had moved to Albany in the early 1940s from Miller County, Georgia. In Albany, he lived on the "fringe" of an African American neighborhood and had few frills as a child. "We came up pretty tough," he said. He had African American playmates as a young boy, but fully understood for most of his players at Graves Springs there would be resistance to Grady and the coming racial and cultural changes that he represented. "It was natural for some of the white kids to have racist attitudes," Cook said. "They were brought up that way."

During one meal at camp, Grady sat down at a table where a group of players was eating. As he did so, all the players at the table got up and moved to another table. Cook saw this and moved from his table to sit with Grady. It was a visible sign of support from the team's white coach toward the lone African American player. "I admired Coach Cook. I knew the kind of pressure he was under from the white people in the community not to accept me," Grady said. "He reached out to me and helped make it easier for other black players who followed me."

After the incident in the dining hall when Cook sat with Grady, "things got better" and players began to accept him, Grady said.

Part of the reason for that was Grady's own tenacity on the football field, his fellow teammates and coaches said. "Once the white kids found out Grady could play, he was accepted," Cook said.

One of those white players who were among the first to accept Grady was Phil Franklin, a team leader, a quarterback who also played defensive back. Phil would later become a bank executive in Albany, but at Grave Springs in the mid-1960s when Grady joined the team, his initial feelings toward him was one of "hostility." Phil said his "southern upbringing" was challenged by the fact that for the first time an African American player had joined the Albany High Indians' football team. The team had been successful in recent years, even winning a state championship in 1959. The players themselves took great pride in their team, and townsfolk by the thousands filled their football stadium to watch them play in the fall. African American fans attended those games but sat in segregated areas. Now Grady was doing something that Phil Franklin did not want to accept. But that would change, too.

"You felt like you weren't supposed to like him," Phil said. "But Grady was such a good guy you couldn't help but like him."

Grady said it was Phil who was one of the first players to offer him a sense of "camaraderie" at Graves Springs and supported him when the regular season had begun. During one game in 1965, Grady was being taunted by some opposing players who were calling him "nigger" and threatening to hurt him. Phil and some of his teammates, the same ones who weeks earlier had tried to run Grady off, now "rallied" to his defense during that game when racial epithets were being hurled at him. "When Phil and some of the others supported me during that game, I felt a part of the team then," Grady said.

Years after Grady broke the color barrier in high school sports in Albany, Phil said the presence of Grady at camp and on the team for two years led to changing attitudes among many white players.

"You didn't have association with them (African Americans) before Graves Springs and football," Phil said. What some white players learned at camp was that "they're just like us."

Phil Franklin and his teammates weren't the only ones reassessing their values after Grady survived the two-week football camp. Grady was learning from that experience at football camp. He was learning about himself and others.

"Graves Springs taught me I could do anything I put my mind to. It also taught me that white people are not as bad as I perceived them to be," Grady said. "That helped break some of the false beliefs that I developed over the years."

His first season was not without some racial harassment from his own team. When the team returned from camp and school had begun, players changed into their practice uniforms in the locker room at the stadium next to the Albany High School campus. One afternoon as Grady was changing clothes, he opened his locker and found a large, dead rattlesnake. He became angry immediately. He grabbed his helmet in one hand and hit "the first white player" he saw. The boy he hit was one of the student managers.

"I remember feeling bad about what I did. I apologized to the boy I hit," Grady said. "I was trying to establish boundaries. I was the only black person on the team."

Once during the 1965 season, the team was traveling out of town to play and stopped at a restaurant to eat. When the owners of the restaurant saw Grady, they spoke with Coach Harold Dean Cook, telling him they would not serve Grady. Cook, his coaches and all the white players were welcomed, but not an African American. Cook refused the service altogether in support of his lone African American player. The team left that restaurant as Cook instructed, and they found a place where all of them, including Grady, could eat together.

For two years Grady was a contributing member of that football team, playing mostly defensive back and at limited times running back. During his senior season in 1966, the team won eight of 10 games and at camp that year things had gone "very smooth" in terms of his relationship with his teammates, Grady said. There were no racial slurs, at least not to his face. He had been accepted because of his determination, character, and contribution on the field. "I had respect, the second year at camp. And I always gave respect," Grady said. At Graves Springs Football Camp in 1966, it was a white player who taught him how to play chess. Things had changed.

About 20 years before Grady broke the color barrier on Albany High's football team, *The Albany Herald* stated that "Negro Leaders" had appeared before the all-white City Commission complaining of over-crowded and deplorable conditions of some "Negro schools." A few years earlier a report from the state government indicated an average of 67 African American students per classroom and 34 for white students. At that City Commission meeting, Joe Watson was the group spokesman and he had lived in Albany for 75 years. He said half of the African American children in the city are "romping the streets, growing up in vice and crime. These will become criminals you will have to contend with in the future."

While African Americans in Albany were given fewer educational opportunities than whites, they had reason to cheer for one of their own, Alice Coachmen who was not becoming a criminal but an international sports star. Coachman, who earned $.50 for every 100 pounds of cotton she picked as a child, won a gold medal in the high jump during the 1948 Olympic Games in London. She became the first African American woman to win a gold medal for the United States.

Grady was not without athletic models growing up in Albany. Only after he graduated from Albany High in 1967 did he come to fully understand that what he had accomplished by integrating the team resonated beyond his own life experiences. He said he came to believe, as others agreed, that his presence on the team ultimately helped both races view one another in more humane ways. Many other African American players would join the Albany High team following Grady's path. By the mid-1960s in Albany, winning high school football games was beginning to take precedent over generations of racial division. He had helped forge a monumental change in Albany. In the beginning, from his own perspective, he didn't see it that way. "I wasn't doing it to be big," Grady said. "To me it wasn't that big of a deal."

For his surrogate father, Dr. William Anderson, it *was* a big deal. Anderson had moved from Albany by the time Grady had joined the Albany High team, but he was kept informed of Grady's accomplishments. Anderson understood the full meaning of what Grady had done. "I think high school sports played a vital role in the process of integration," Anderson said. It brought the races together and by its very nature required common effort, sacrifice to the team and not the individual. Anderson compared Grady to another Georgia-born athlete, Jackie Robinson, who by the late 1940s had become the first African American to integrate modern major league baseball. For both Jackie Robinson and Grady Caldwell their decisions were not without risks to their own personal safety from whites resisting these changes. "Grady was the one who broke the barrier in Albany," Anderson said. "Those who were the first in this arena bore the brunt of pent up hostility."

* * *

When Grady began his senior year, his girlfriend, Kathleen, decided to transfer from Monroe to begin her junior year at Albany High. It was not just to be with Grady. Kathleen's mother, Lois, had wanted her daughter to transfer and said she'd likely be challenged more academically, have newer textbooks, and better facilities than she had at Monroe High School. Kathleen said Lois Jones was right. Kathleen experienced other things, too.

She confronted racial slurs, meanness, and degrading treatment from some of the white students and from at least one teacher, Mr. N. C. Hatcher, who taught history. In Hatcher's class, he allowed his students to use racial slurs toward Kathleen and other African American students. When Kathleen had his class, she was the only African American student, and he routinely used the word "negra" in front of the class and allowed whites to say "nigger" in reference to Kathleen.

"I hated that room. Some days, a lot of days, I just wanted to quit and go back to Monroe," Kathleen said.

Neither she nor Grady were physically hurt while at Albany High. The abuse came in the form of being ostracized, intimidated and verbally attacked by some of the white students. There were physical fights between some African Americans and whites at Albany High during this initial period of integration, but they were not involved in any. Pennies were sometimes thrown at Kat and other African Americans as they walked the halls of the school going from class to class. It was said to be symbolic of what some whites felt about the worthiness of their new classmates. "On some occasions I felt inadequate about being around white people. But sometimes I'd rise and stand my ground," Kathleen said.

One of those times was when Lois Jones urged her daughter to rise and make a stand in her history class by asking her teacher to stop using the word "negra" and use the word Negro. Lois wanted her children to strike back even if it was in small ways, like trying to order an ice cream cone from the front of Arctic Bear and not the back. Kathleen in the beginning was scared to talk to Hatcher about his language and that of her classmates. She later found the strength to do it.

"I told Mr. Hatcher that the word is pronounced 'Negro' not 'negra.' My mom told me to tell him how to pronounce it," Kathleen said.

The conversation Kathleen had with her teacher did not change what he did and said in class and what he allowed white students to say. Once when Hatcher was absent from school, a substitute teacher reported to Kathleen's history class. That day in class students were reading their current events reports out loud and one student said "negra" as the report was being read. The substitute, a woman, challenged that student who used that word. "The sub said, 'It's pronounced Negro, and if you can't say it right, don't say it at all.' I felt like a queen that day," Kathleen said.

The name calling, the harassment would continue throughout her days at Albany High until she graduated in 1968. There were a few whites, very few, who did reach out to her. One was Martha Glenn Riley, whose nickname was "Duster." She was brought up in a family that was more "opened minded about race" and integration than most of her white contemporaries, Martha Glenn said. Her view was the new African

American students were an overall "asset" to the school, especially good athletes like Grady Caldwell.

Martha Glenn played on the girls' basketball team, which would include African American players by the end of the 1960s. She was called a "nigger-lover" by some of the whites who resented her associating and befriending Kathleen and other African American students. "It was pitiful the way they (African American students) were treated. It was like they had some disease," Martha Glenn said.

The relationship between Martha Glenn and Kathleen Jones that was formed at Albany High in those turbulent days endures today. "Even to this day when she sees me, she hugs me," Kathleen said.

There is one compelling and longstanding vision that lives on in Martha Glenn's mind about Kathleen Jones and Grady Caldwell and those days at Albany High. "The thing that stands out to me is seeing Grady and Kathleen walking down the hall together," Martha Glenn said. "You'd always see those smiles. God guided them through and gave them strength."

Kathleen attended Albany High football games to watch Grady play and during one game she took her younger brother Stephen, who was about six at the time. During that game Grady scored a touchdown, and when he did, Stephen jumped from his seat and said, "I love to see that little nigger run!" In embarrassment, Kathleen held her head down after hearing her brother's cheer. They had been sitting among a throng of white faces at the stadium. "They had been calling us niggers at school," Kathleen said. She's able to laugh about that many years later.

During the 1966-67 school year, with Kat now enrolled at Albany High, and she and Grady dating, he picked her up on the way to school each morning in a four-door white Valiant, a car that Grady's mother had bought him. Kat did not have a car, and her mother tried to convince Kat to ride the bus to school with other students. She wanted to be with Grady. After he picked up Kat, Grady then drove to Holly Homes public housing and picked up his friend, Robert Thomas, Jr., whose nickname was "Bob-Bob." Robert had transferred to Albany High the same year Grady did. They rode down Davis Street then onto Residence Avenue where the imposing redbrick high school covered a full block. Robert gave Grady a dollar each week for gas and rode in the backseat. Kathleen sat in the front and rode for free. This was their routine each morning. "I always picked Kat up first even though Bob-Bob was closer to my house. I made sure she rode up front next to me," Grady said.

There were many times during those morning rides to school when Kathleen thought it wasn't worth the anxiety and humiliation she was suffering as a student at Albany High. During her first few months at school, she thought almost daily about leaving Albany High and returning to Monroe. She found the strength to keep going. She prayed during school and at night, asking God to give her the strength she needed. She found comfort and solace in her relationship with God. Grady helped her, talked to her about being strong and continuing what she had started in order to become an Albany High graduate, which she did. Sometimes it was Robert who was able to divert Kathleen's mind to other subjects than what she was enduring at school. Robert loved to talk and gossip. Each morning when he got into the car, Grady said Robert started the day with this phrase, "Grady, let me tell you..."

After that, Robert would tell Grady and Kathleen the latest social gossip, political news, and other nuggets he had overheard at his father's business, Harlem Barber Shop. At that barber shop, men talked and Robert listened. What Robert heard he would eventually tell Grady and Kathleen on the way to Albany High in the backseat of that white Valiant. One morning Robert began his pontificating on the way to school and said something that Kathleen disagreed with. She said something back to him that he disagreed with. Robert said he knew he was right and she was wrong. An argument ensued. It became heated, and Kathleen slapped Robert and he slapped her, neither one hitting the other in the face or head. No one was hurt. But Grady had had enough by then. "I couldn't believe they were fighting like that," Grady said. "I had to stop my car on the way to school and make them stop. We later laughed about it."

The three of them could not recall the source of the argument, only that it was harmless and occurred on the way to school. Robert did recall an incident at school that potentially could've been harmful to his physical safety. They didn't laugh about that when it was over. This occurred when he and Grady were juniors. That day Grady did not have football practice, and Robert was to ride home from school with him. Robert was waiting for him next to his car while Grady was inside the school building making up a test for one of his classes. When Grady left the building and was walking toward his car, he saw trouble. He saw the mob.

Robert was standing next to Grady's car, but there were about "20 to 25 white boys" who had encircled him. They were shouting racial threats at Robert. He was scared. Grady kept a leather strap in his car and at the end of the strap was a large rock. It was in his car to be used to defend Grady and his friends if they were threatened by others. Robert was threatened that day and had gotten the leather strap out of the car and was holding it in his right hand. The racial threats continued. Robert became more scared. Then he saw Grady walking through the parking lot toward him and the gang of white students.

"I had that leather strap in my hand and Grady walked up to me and took it. He put it back in the car," Robert said. "Those boys started backing off a little when they saw Grady. They respected him more because he played football. I didn't play football." Robert said.

"I broke through that crowd and said, 'If you want to jump on someone, jump on me.' I could get away with more because I played football," Grady said. "After I said that, they left Bob-Bob alone and we got in our car and went home."

For Bob-Bob and his two years at Albany High before graduating with Grady in 1967, that afternoon in the parking lot surrounded by all those white students was the most fearful experience he had at the school. Like the other African American students, he tolerated daily indignities. He was called awful racist names, spit balls were thrown at him, and he and other African American students tried to sit in the back of the classrooms. "We would get in the back so we could see what was going on. The teachers knew that some of the white kids would do about anything to us during class. It wasn't awful every day, but it could be bad," Robert said.

One teacher, Mary Jo Hogg, was remembered by Robert as someone who treated him decently. She taught bookkeeping and according to Robert, "loved the football players. She never gave me any problems because she knew Grady and I were friends. She treated me like she did Grady," Robert said.

At lunch Robert, Grady, and other African American students usually had a plan. They would choose one among themselves to get their food and sit at a table with a group of white students. When the African American student sat down, the whites would leave the table with their trays and sometimes sit on the floor to finish lunch instead of eating with the African American student. When the white students left the table, other African American students would get their trays and sit at the table to eat lunch. The quality of the food at Albany High was better than they were used to, Robert said.

"They had some of the best food we ever had. We thought we had died and gone to heaven during lunch," Robert said. "We had all this different food to pick from. At Monroe it was just one thing. And everything they served at Albany High was good."

Good food wasn't the reason Robert transferred to Albany High the same year Grady did. His father, Robert Thomas, Sr., who had been a leader in the Albany Civil Rights Movement, encouraged his son and two daughters to transfer to Albany High for better educational opportunities. Janice Thomas would remain a student at Monroe, while Robert's other sister, Joyce Loette, would become an Albany High graduate too.

"Our dad talked to us about transferring and what we thought about going to Albany High. He didn't force us," Robert said. "He knew it would be tough. But he thought we would get a better overall education. When I look back at it all, he was right."

Robert remembers that humiliation and pain from being an Albany High student for two years. He was a good basketball player growing up and had planned to try out for the Albany High team his junior year. There were a few other African Americans who were going out for the team that year. Tryouts had been originally scheduled by the basketball coach for after school. Robert said the coach then changed the time to six in the morning, expecting the African American athletes not to come. Robert and the other African Americans students found out about the time change and attended the tryouts.

"Not a black player made that team. The list came out and we were all cut," Robert said. "I was good enough to make it, and there were others too. It just wasn't fair."

He did not tryout again his senior year. Soon African American players would break the color barrier on that team as Grady had done for football. After graduating from Albany High, Robert enrolled at Albany State College and earned a degree in business administration in 1971. He met his future wife there, Barbara Floyd from Jesup, Georgia. They've been married for more than 40 years and have one son together. For about 20 years he worked as a contract negotiator at Robins Air Force Base in Warner Robins, Georgia. He retired from that position and began running fulltime his own business, Thomas Insurance Services. Barbara has taught elementary school for nearly 40 years.

"I felt great when I graduated from Albany High. Me and Grady and the rest of us always said that if we got that diploma, we'd never go back to that school. We still had a lot of bad memories," Robert said.

Robert, Grady, and some of the other African Americans who graduated in 1967 did not return to the school until the summer of 2010 when they were invited there by school administrators to see the ongoing school renovation. The school was changing, but the real change had come in the 1960s when Robert and Grady had been students there. They had made those changes possible.

* * *

Grady and Kathleen were dating throughout their high school years with Kathleen remaining faithful to him, in love with him, and not wanting to be with another boy. It wasn't the same for Grady. He had relationships with other girls, brief sexual encounters and one that resulted in pregnancy and the birth of Grady's first child. "I had always been a womanizer. Even back in high school when I dated Kat," Grady said.

Without Kathleen knowing it, Grady had been spending time with Annie Kate Graham, a high school student a year older than Grady. Annie Kate became pregnant and a daughter, Yolanda, was born to her and Grady in 1966. When Kathleen found out she was furious. Grady's initial reaction was to "deny paternity," he said and he did that for a while. It would be years before he even saw his child.

"I was so hurt when it happened. I couldn't believe it. At first I didn't believe it, and I didn't want Grady to have anything to do with that child," Kathleen said. "I regretted that and later apologized to Yolanda for the way I was back then."

It would be years later before Grady himself apologized to Yolanda for his behavior as a teen-age father in the 1960s. The two would eventually reconcile. As with others in Grady's family, Yolanda would suffer emotionally because of what Grady did and what he had failed to do. Grady's struggle for redemption would be long and difficult. Many hearts would ache along the journey.

FOUR

Grady Caldwell and Kathleen Jones were married March 18, 1969, at Bethel AME Church on Washington Street and Highland Avenue where Kathleen had attended with her family, gone to Sunday school, and accepted Jesus Christ as her Lord and Savior. It was a hopeful day full of prayers and God's blessings. The two had been talking about getting married for some time and had set an earlier date than expected after learning Kathleen was pregnant with Grady's child. Daphne Caldwell was born November 6, 1969, and she would be the first of three children for the couple. Kathleen's church and her faith in God had played a pivotal role in her childhood and would be the foundation she would turn to in the years ahead when the troubles began for Grady and their family. She would hold on hard to it. She would have to.

After Daphne was born, for a short period they lived with Lois Jones, Kathleen's mother, on Whitney Avenue. Kathleen had enrolled at Albany State after graduating from Albany High in 1968, and Grady had already begun attending college there by the summer of 1967. They had strong family support, and they were both determined to earn college degrees. Before attending Albany State, Grady was offered a full athletic scholarship at South Carolina State University. If accepted, Grady would've played football and joined the school's swim team. Grady said he was unwilling to give up his car in order to accept the scholarship offer.

"They had a policy that freshmen couldn't keep a car on campus.

Looking back on that, it was pretty stupid of me to not have taken that scholarship," Grady said.

Grady would for a period join the Albany State swim team, but eventually, while still a student, he took a fulltime job working at the Firestone plant in Albany. The tire maker began production in Albany by the late 1960s. After about a year living with Kathleen's mother, the young family moved out and rented an apartment on Hickory Lane. Things were going well. Kathleen and Grady were both pursuing college degrees, and Grady was working and making "good money" at Firestone, "around $300 a week," he said. Grady took morning classes and came home for lunch and worked three to eleven at Firestone. He worked in the warehouse and eventually was promoted to supervisor. He worked hard. It was the same way he did on the football field at Graves Springs Camp.

Grady had never been a partier or big drinker during high school and into his first couple of years in college. That changed. His Firestone job provided the money he needed to support his family and the dignity that comes when hard work is accomplished. The job gave him something else. Grady and some of his co-workers were paid every Thursday, and they went together after work that day to cash their checks at a liquor store in east Albany in an area known as Five Points. He cashed his check and began buying liquor with his co-workers. This was the beginning. Grady didn't know it then; neither did Kathleen.

"That was my idea of a man. Everybody was working hard and we drank hard," Grady said. "I started off buying a half pint and before long I was buying half gallons. Drinking after getting off work at Firestone was the beginning of my addictive behavior."

Grady became a heavy weekend drinker while earning a degree in business administration in 1971. He bought bourbon, Benchmark and sometimes Maker's Mark, when he finished his shift at Firestone. He drank it with Coca-Cola, sometimes more liquor than Coke. He got drunk a lot during the weekends. Kathleen didn't like the drinking, wasn't a drinker herself, but she tolerated it in the beginning. He continued to work and provide for his family.

"I enjoyed the euphoric feeling from alcohol. I didn't like the hangovers, but I was the life of the party," Grady said. "And I enjoyed being the life of the party."

Grady had found something else he liked during that period of heavy drinking and partying. It was during his junior year at Albany State when one of his boyhood friends, Larry McCartherens, who had gone to college in Knoxville, Tennessee, returned to Albany to visit and offered marijuana to Grady. That was the first time he smoked "good marijuana," he said. He got stoned, real stoned. He enjoyed it. Before that experience he had tried the drug a few times but didn't use it regularly. After getting high with his friend home from college, Grady wanted more marijuana. He would find ways to get it. "That was the first time I smoked what I thought was really good pot," Grady said. "This started me on my drug habit. Cocaine would be next."

He wanted more marijuana, and he wanted more money than what Firestone was paying him. He quit the job with the tire maker and said he wanted "to be rich" and later became involved in a business venture known as "Dare to be Great." This was a pyramid-based financial arrangement in which Grady sold cosmetics for a few years after leaving his job at Firestone. He would work both in the Atlanta area and

Birmingham before leaving this venture and returning to Albany. "I made some money, but I blew a lot of money, too," Grady said. "I ended up living in the Atlanta area. I left my family in Albany for a while."

Kathleen had not been pleased with his career decisions. "I didn't want Grady to leave Firestone and the security we had, but he did. He thought he was going to be rich," Kathleen said. "I was already concerned about him. I knew he was drinking a lot on the weekends and smoking dope."

By the early 1970s, Kathleen had graduated from Albany State, and she and Daphne eventually joined Grady in Atlanta living in the Sandy Springs area. Not long after their move into an apartment complex, a fire broke out. None of the Caldwells were injured, but that was enough to convince her to return to Albany with Daphne. She did not like the big city life. Grady continued to work selling cosmetics for a period but eventually quit and returned to Albany to rejoin his family. In Albany Kathleen accepted a job with Albany State College in the same office she had worked in as a student before moving to Atlanta. She would work for Albany State College fulltime for more than 30 years. During this period Albany State College became Albany State University. Her tenure included financial aid counselor and later she was promoted to director of recruitment, admissions and financial aid. Her final ten years at the university she worked solely as director of financial aid. Working at Albany State provided a long period of financial stability for her family. She retired with a strong reputation for service and professionalism recognized by her colleagues over several years. Her husband's life would turn in another direction.

FIVE

In 1974 Grady ran for the Albany City Commission, a body politic that had been all-white, marking the long era of Jim Crow and racism in the Deep South. He lost to incumbent B. C. Gable in November of that year, and the following month Grady was one of four African Americans from Dougherty County listed as plaintiffs in a federal landmark suit seeking to strike down at-large voting during city-wide elections. At-large voting was one method used by whites to keep African Americans from being elected. Now for the first time it was going to be tested in federal court.

Only 25 years old, Grady was encouraged by local African American leaders to run, including attorney C. B. King who had long been politically active in Albany, playing an important role during the 1960s Civil Rights Movement. Grady said he felt honored that fellow African Americans viewed him with such leadership potential. He had faith then in his own abilities, was confident, and well spoken. People listened to him despite his youthfulness.

"I ran to impact the system. At that point I was heavily involved with community activities," Grady said. "And I was well known throughout the African American community in Albany."

Kathleen saw it differently. She had mixed views about Grady's decision to run for the Albany City Commission. She knew that his personal life included at times heavy drinking and smoking dope. These are not assets for any long-term political career.

"I was excited at one level and very cautious at another level. I didn't really think he was ready for it," Kathleen said. "To me he was being pushed. He was just too young. I didn't want the limelight."

Mary Young, a local African American attorney, had run and been defeated for the City Commission herself in 1972, "was pushing Grady to run," Kathleen said. Young would by the late 1970s be elected to the Commission with Grady serving as her campaign manager, all made possible by the federal lawsuit on their behalf. The other two plaintiffs were Fanny Paige and Erma Moss. The suit stated the present ward boundaries "minimize the effectiveness of black voters – depriving plaintiffs of rights secured by the Fourteenth and Fifteenth Amendments." Both amendments were ratified after the Civil War ended in 1865 giving African Americans full citizenship and voting rights. Southern white resistance, and the lack of federal enforcement of these amendments, had historically marginalized African Americans in Albany and elsewhere. The suit named Mayor James H. Gray, Sr., four other members of the City Commission, and Dougherty Registrar-Elections Supervisor Donald Pye. As with the mid-1960s at Albany High, Grady again was shaping local history.

At-large voting was given legal standing in the 1940s by the Georgia General Assembly to diminish African American political strength. It was in accordance of an old southern white political strategy using a new tactic. During the hearing, Grady testified in federal court in what was described in *The Albany Herald* August 6, 1975, as the "first-of-its kind" voting suit in the nation. City Attorney James Davis fought the suit, declaring Albany "has been a progressive city...not discriminating against anybody."

To accept fully this premise you would have to be oblivious of history. It is always possible.

Federal Judge Wilbur Owens in Macon, who earlier had ordered the desegregation of Dougherty County Schools, presided over the hearing and said he "will permit this to proceed as a class action" on behalf of all African Americans. By the end of the month Owens had ruled in favor of Grady and the other plaintiffs, eventually eliminating at-large City Commission elections and replacing them with ward voting. The city did appeal the ruling to the 5th Circuit Court of Appeals, but it upheld Owens' decision. This soon led to the elections of Mary Young and other African American civil rights leader. Many African Americans in Albany were watching closely the leadership of the youthful Grady Caldwell.

Grady's role in electoral politics was short, but it was a contribution that proved dramatic in advancing equality for African Americans in Albany. Another piece of segregationist history had ended. Judge Owens, based on *The Albany Herald,* said the 1947 General Assembly law approving Albany's at-large system of electing its officials "had the inevitable effect of abridging the right of Negro citizens of Albany to vote and it therefore violative of their rights under the 15th Amendment."

"I was just fortunate to be involved in that lawsuit. It did help change the city for the better," Grady said. "But I learned later on politics was not my forte. God was calling me in another direction." He would not seek public office again. That was the mid-1970s, and it would be years before Grady reached the place God wanted him to be.

Grady's involvement in the federal lawsuit and the fact he became the first African American to integrate Albany High's football team in the mid-1960s reflect an enormous contribution to Albany at a very young age.

Dr. Lee Formwalt, former director of the Organization of American Historians, said the actions by Grady and the other plaintiffs of the suit have had far reaching influence on city politics and southern history. "It changed everything. The nature of local politics was significantly different" after Judge Owens ruled on behalf of Grady and the three other plaintiffs. Before becoming director of the OAH, Formwalt spent about 20 years teaching history at Albany State University and doing extensive research on local and southern history. Following his career at OAH in Bloomington, Indiana, Formwalt returned to Albany and became the executive director of the Albany Civil Rights Institute. By the end of 2011 he had resigned his job at the Institute and returned to Indiana where he had begun writing a memoir. I have known and admired Lee for several years and during one period I wrote for and helped edit a publication he started called the *Southwest Georgia Journal of History*. The Owens' ruling would have profound changes in terms of promoting civil rights in Albany, Formwalt said.

"Think about this: For the first time in local history you have African Americans serving on the City Commission after the ruling by the federal court," Formwalt said. "I don't believe there was anything like that during Reconstruction."

For a short period after the Civil War ended in 1865, US troops were sent to Georgia and throughout the South, providing safety to African Americans voting and running for office for the first time in history. They needed protection from the Ku Klux Klan, the white racist organization formed after the war and noted for its use of terror and violence to keep African Americans from voting. During Reconstruction, Formwalt said, African Americans from Dougherty County and throughout Georgia served in the state General Assembly. There were no African Americans then elected to local offices in Albany. Soon, when the federal troops were removed and with the Klan in charge, there would be no more African Americans elected to statewide offices. The lawsuit Grady was involved in by the 1970s would change a hundred years of bitter history. Eliminating at-large elections and replacing them with ward voting allowed African Americans to elect one another to the City Commission and was "an outstanding contribution" to the civil rights movement, he said.

"So the fact that blacks finally had a voice in local government was a very significant change," Formwalt said. "It was 14 years after King left Albany and after the desegregation of schools. It *was* done and it took federal action to do it."

* * *

Lee Formwalt reminded me of another important civil rights lawsuit from Albany that was filed in federal court by the mid-1970s. Johnnie Johnson was an African American sanitation worker for the city of Albany during that period, and he organized a strike of about 260 African Americans sanitation and public utility workers. Johnson and few other workers sued the city government for equitable rights and pay. In the early 1970s the city government refused to allow African American workers to apply for promotions, had segregated restrooms and water fountains, and even had segregated employee functions such as Christmas parties. Institutional racism had not been entirely cleansed from the culture.

As was the case with Grady's lawsuit, Judge Wilbur Owens ruled on behalf of Johnson and his fellow workers. These two suits were both landmark cases, Formwalt said. In 2012 the Albany City Commission voted to name its public works building after Johnnie Johnson.

By the late 1970s Grady had been elected president of the Congress of Black Organizations, a coalition of about 25 members that included African American civic and social organizations throughout Albany. Its purpose was to promote opportunities and equality for African Americans. On August 1, 1979, *The Albany Herald* included a story, accompanied by a photograph of Grady wearing a jacket and tie, indicating the CBO was organizing a voter registration drive with a goal of 5,000 new voters. The paper quoted Grady.

"This is the first time an organized, intensive effort has been made (to register voters) since the Albany Movement..." He said a successful drive would give the African American community "leverage" in political circles more in proportion to its "potential."

The story also included quotes from the local president of the National Association for the Advancement of Colored People, which was working alongside Grady and the CBO to promote the voter registration drive. The newspaper article ended with another quote from Grady. "I'm certain that we can make a difference, we will be heard. Particularly in those districts that we have a high concentration of blacks."

During the late 1970s, as Mary Young was serving on the City Commission, she nominated Grady to serve on the Southwest Georgia

Planning and Development Commission. He accepted that post for a short period. By the mid-1980s, though, the political activism and promise of Grady Caldwell had ended. Drugs were becoming more important to his life by then.

SIX

The Caldwell's second child, Carmen, was born in 1976, and Grady was working with the Federation of Southern Cooperatives in Albany, which was a federally-funded program designed to provide assistance to African American farmers. He was searching for the right fit. His liquor drinking and marijuana usage had not stopped. There were girlfriends, too. Kathleen would know about them later when things got worse. She would learn about her husband, his drug addiction, and other women. It would all break her heart.

By the early 1980s Grady inquired about a job at Albany State College through one of his mentors when he had been a student there. Dr. C. W. Grant was dean of students then and needed to fill the position for director of student activities. He was excited when he learned Grady was interested in the job. Grant had hired Kathleen and remembered Grady fondly when he had been a student at Albany State. Grant said Grady had been a "student leader," kept better than average grades, had earned the respect from his peers and the faculty. When Grady did graduate from Albany State, Grant had predicted that whatever path he chose, he would do well. Other people who knew Grady back then would've said the same. In the beginning when Grady was hired, Grant said he knew he had made the right choice.

Kathleen and Grady were now both employed at Albany State, making good salaries. Financially, they were stable. They bought their first home together during this period at 1121 St. Andrews Street in a comfortable middle-class area in southwest Albany. It was a neighborhood where other African Americans and white professionals lived. Grady had "sold the home to myself" having gotten a real estate license through a local realty company. Their third child, Grady Lee Caldwell III, had been born in 1980. Grady had a wife who loved him and was devoted to him and their children. Now he had a son to carry on the Caldwell name. That son and his two daughters would have a father, unlike Grady who lost his when he was young. Grady then was determined to see that through. While working at Albany State, Grady found another father figure, like he had had in Dr. William Anderson during the early 1960s.

"I viewed him as a very, very competent protégé. Grady had a very good mind. He still has a very good mind," Grant said. "It was more of a father and son relationship for us. He used to travel a lot with me. He was in my fraternity."

Grant was born in Jacksonville, Florida, in 1931, and in 1966 was hired by Albany State as director of student activities and dormitory counselor. He had attended Florida A & M in Tallahassee, and his wife, Velma, was hired by Albany State College to teach English. Grant had not planned to stay long in Albany. When he got there, that changed. He was later promoted to dean of students. He enjoyed both the college and community and was active in helping both for many years. Grant retired from Albany State in 1996, but twice since then he had served as interim vice-president for student affairs. He played a key role in establishing a civil rights museum in Albany in the 1990s. Today it's referred to as the Albany Civil Rights Institute. The museum was first housed in Mt. Zion Baptist Church on Whitney Avenue, the same place Dr. King spoke during the early 1960s. It was the same church Grady attended when he was a boy and into manhood. Mt. Zion was where he had accepted Jesus as his Savior. Grady was about to embark on a dark time when it seemed that nothing, not even God, could save him.

One of the things Grady did as director of student activities was to help Grant promote the Kappa Alapha Psi fraternity. Grant was responsible for working with chapters in and outside of Georgia. The two often traveled together, spending nights on the road. Grady had been a member of that same fraternity while he was a student at Albany State. His first threat to his own life and to the lives of others happened while he was a pledge to that fraternity. Grady was sent to Florida A & M by Grant, the fraternity's advisor, to learn how to dance and perform with a cane. That wasn't the only thing Grady did down in Tallahassee.

"We were partying and I was drunk and had been smoking marijuana. I had a Pontiac LeMans and totaled my car," Grady said. "One of my frat brothers was with me. I hit a couple of trees and my frat brother had to have stiches in his face, and spent the night in the hospital. That was my first experience of getting in trouble. But more trouble was on the way."

Still, Grant and others who knew Grady as a student and later as a college graduate seeking to make his mark in this world viewed the incident in Tallahassee as an isolated one, a bad decision by a college student. Grady was not hurt during the wreck. He had some minor criminal charges. He said he believed then, and others said the same, he had learned his lesson and he would not again put himself and others in such a dangerous situation. They would all be wrong.

Before that drunken wreck in Tallahassee, the first time Grady had gotten into any trouble with the law was April 4, 1968, the night Dr. Martin Luther King, Jr. was assassinated in Memphis, Tennessee. He told his mother something that night but didn't mean it. "I told my momma that night after we heard the news that I was going to jail," Grady said.

He was angry, if not mad, and hurt like many others who had come to know and admire Dr. King, a man Grady had spent time with years before. What Grady had said to Leola that night was out of a sense of painful loss, and not because he had intended to do something foolish. Later in the evening Grady got in his car and drove to Gray's Chicken Box on the corner of Corn Avenue and Newton Road. Gray's Chicken Box was a favorite restaurant in the neighborhood, and it served hamburgers and fried chicken. The owner could be cantankerous but the food was great, Kathleen said. After Grady got his food, he backed his car onto the road into the path of an oncoming police vehicle.

"The police stopped me and said I slowed them up from an emergency call. I got angry after that. I said some things I shouldn't have," Grady said.

"Grady flipped out that night," Kathleen said.

The police handcuffed Grady and took him to the police station and placed him in a jail cell. He was not charged with a crime. His mother was telephoned, came immediately to the police station, and Grady was released to her. That night in Albany African Americans cried, prayed, but there were no outbreaks of violence or riots. It wasn't that way in other cities. In more than 100 American cities rioting occurred, killing approximately 39 people and injuring about 2,500. By the time the night had ended, there were more than 75,000 National Guardsmen and federal troops on the streets of those cities. There was reason enough to cry for America.

"My momma got me out of jail that night. She got her baby out of jail," Grady said. It would be Leola he would turn to, time and time again, when drug addiction and his criminal life would cause Kathleen to kick Grady out of the house. Jail time would come. Then prison. Unlike the night Dr. King was murdered, in the years ahead there'd be reasons enough to put Grady behind bars. By the time Grant had hired Grady as director of student activities at Albany State, the notion that he would self-destruct through a cocaine habit and become a petty thief was as unpredictable as the night Grady was handcuffed at Gray's Chicken Box.

SEVEN

Grady's tenure under Grant began well. He was promoted to director of alumni affairs. After the first couple of years in this new position, Grant said he and others at the college began to notice a change in Grady's work habits. He got sloppy. In the beginning he was punctual for events. Then he began showing up unprepared ten, 15 or even 20 minutes late for important meetings and events. This worried Grant. Even before that promotion, Grant was beginning to doubt and question the young man with so much promise. The young man that he had mentored over the years was "slipping," Grant said.

One weekend before Grady had secured his promotion, he and Grant traveled to South Carolina together to help promote their fraternity, Kappa Alpha Psi. When they returned to Albany, Grady asked Grant if he could borrow his car for a day or two. Grant agreed. Grady returned the car on a Monday and "it was just filthy," Grant said. He took the car to a car wash, left it and picked it up later. The car was cleaned, but those who did the work found part of a marijuana joint in the car and placed it on the ashtray, allowing Grant to see it. He found the drug.

"I confronted Grady, and he didn't deny it. And I said, 'I can't afford to take a chance with you. I can't take you out of town with me again,' " Grant said.

This experience rattled Grady. He refocused himself at work and managed to get the promotion to director of alumni affairs despite the fact that Dr. Grant knew full well of his drug usage. Grady did not stop using drugs, nor drinking heavily. He hid it better and secured the promotion. Grady said he knew the promotion "pissed C. W. off" because Grant knew that Grady was now living a life of heavy drinking and drug use. The promotion came anyway.

"I could function with the marijuana and liquor during that period. Then I got into the cocaine, and it wasn't long before I couldn't function at all," Grady said.

That period Grady referred to was the early 1980s. It was then he began to associate with Rev. Robert E. Hines, a local minister and teacher who exposed Grady to freebased cocaine. He even smoked during working hours at Albany State. There were other professionals in Albany he was getting stoned with away from campus, Grady said. But the first to offer him freebased cocaine was Rev. Hines. A 20-year cocaine addiction began. It would almost kill Grady. There'd be some days he thought he was dead.

"Sometimes at work I'd tell my secretary not to disturb me, and I closed the door and smoked in my office. I'd come out of there with sweat rolling off my face. I don't know how many times I did that," Grady said. "I can't remember. I can't remember a lot of things back then because of the drugs I took. After a while people at the college knew what I was doing. I couldn't hide the cocaine like I did marijuana."

Kathleen's office was in the same building and one day he noticed she was upset. Her face couldn't hide the pain that Grady was causing her because of his drug habit. She was suffering herself because of what her husband was doing. Grant went into her office and spoke to her about the situation with Grady. Grady was home that day, she said. He was using cocaine at their home. Both angry and saddened by what was happening to Grady and Kathleen and what he heard that day in her office, Grant left campus and drove to the Caldwell home and found Grady there high on dope and very lethargic. He was a mess, Grant said.

"I got over there to their home and he was just all spaced out," Grant said. "I said to him, 'I'll take you down to the Oglethorpe Bridge and you can jump in the Flint River. You don't have the right to destroy other peoples' lives – you can destroy your own.' "

Grady did not jump off the bridge into the Flint that passes near the Albany State campus. Grant's words, though, were not without some influence. A few days after Grant's visit, Grady was admitted to a rehabilitation clinic in Waycross, Georgia. He stayed for a few weeks, got clean and got out. He stayed clean for a short period after that – then went back to smoking freebased cocaine. There would be other rehab clinics over the next 20 years. He'd go in, get out, stay straight for a while, and then his addictive behavior would begin again.

By 1984 Rev. Robert E. Hines had been convicted of murdering his girlfriend's brother and was sentenced to prison that year. By 2011 he was still incarcerated at the Calhoun State Prison about 30 miles west of Albany. Grady said he had ended his relationship with Hines when the two of them were at Hines' home and Grady noticed that Hines had taken his picture and placed it over the picture of Jesus on his Bible. Grady would no longer be associated with the minister who was sentenced to prison, but the freebased cocaine use, the debauchery, and suicidal behavior would continue for years and years.

"One of the reasons I did cocaine was because I found out what it did to the ladies," Grady said. "I'd lock up with two or three girls in a motel room and let them wear me out, and themselves, too."

Grady's life at home with Kathleen and their three children was crumbling, as was his job at Albany State. At one point Grady's new supervisor Ellen White had scheduled a workshop on leadership and team-building that Grady was expected to attend at the Sheraton Inn, not far from the campus. Grady did not want to go. Heavy was his use of drugs during that period. He had a plan to keep from going to the workshop.

"I told her I had a drug problem and I knew she would have empathy on me," Grady said. "She excused me from the workshop, and I went back to using my drugs that day."

By the mid-1980s some of Grady's friends who had connections with the local police began telling him that law enforcement was beginning to believe that Grady might be selling a substantial amount of cocaine. Grady said he did not sell drugs during that period or any period when he was addicted. For years he bought drugs from suppliers in Sylvester, a small farming town about 20 miles east of Albany.

"I never sold drugs. I did a lot. I was an addict for years," Grady said. "But I never sold cocaine to make money."

Albany State president, Dr. Billy Black, insisted Grady be admitted to another rehabilitation clinic, and this time it was the Satilla Substance Abuse Treatment Center in Waycross, about two hours east of Albany. Black had told Grady if he didn't go and get off the dope, he would be fired from his job or asked to resign. Grady had hope. He said he believed then he would get clean for good. He spent about a month in that facility. Kathleen did not visit him but they did speak over the telephone and exchanged letters during his rehab period.

"I was so angry and frustrated by then. I didn't want to see Grady," Kathleen said. "I didn't go to Waycross when he was there."

From the rehab clinic in Waycross, Grady wrote Kathleen the letter below dated July 23, 1985:

Dear Kat,

The pictures and cards really made my birthday. Tell the kids that for me, even though I know you got them (smile). Things are going well and I did have a good birthday. We ate chicken, and that was what I have been wanting since I have been here.

I was thinking, this was the first birthday in 18 years that I have had without drugs. It wasn't so bad after all. I love you and the kids and thanks for making my day.

Love,
Grady

"When I got out that time, I still had my job. I thought I had this thing whipped," Grady said. "But then Albany State demoted me from director of alumni affairs to a job in institutional advancement. I got pissed off and started freebasing again."

He was allowing the drugs to whip him again. His work suffered and administrators at Albany State made a decision not to fire Grady, but allow him to resign. The pattern continued. Grady "got clean for a while" after he left the college and made some money in "private consulting and motivational speaking," he said. Kathleen by then had been providing most of the family's financial needs. She continued to work at Albany State as director of financial aid, and she struggled to hold her family together by focusing on her children as her husband was slipping further and further into a walking hell. It would not be easy.

Even before Grady's addiction led to his losing his job at Albany State, Kathleen had noticed his paychecks had become "less and less" because he was cashing them, spending his money on drugs, and sometimes there was little left over for the family. At one point she confronted him about the lack of money from his paycheck.

"He admitted to me what it was. See, back then I didn't know anything about drugs and what they could do," Kathleen said. "It took me a long time to believe it was actually happening."

Grady was never physically violent, Kathleen said. He did not verbally abuse Kathleen or the children when using drugs. Grady called himself "an intellectual drug addict" believing he could always handle and quit when he wanted to whether liquor, marijuana, or even cocaine. He was wrong about that. The periods that he'd get clean, sometimes just a few weeks at a time, he would provide his children with the proper love and guidance they needed. He loved them, but he never stayed clean long during the 20-year period. Kathleen tried to shield their children from their father's behavior, the life he was living elsewhere as a drug addict and with women in dirty hotel rooms who gave themselves to Grady as long as he gave them cocaine.

"I may have told Daphne, our oldest, that Daddy had to go get some help. This would've been when he went to Waycross for treatment," Kathleen said. "I just didn't want to talk to them a lot about it."

Kathleen focused on rearing her children and trying to keep things as "normal as possible" in a household where their father might leave for three or four days and return after "a cocaine binge," she said. Kathleen constantly talked to Grady, prayed for him, and tried to get him to quit and stay clean. At one point Grady was using cocaine in the house, and Kathleen became so overcome with emotion, she became hysterical and prostrate "on the floor" begging her husband to stop using drugs. He did not. Things would get worse.

During this period, Grady begin visiting a girlfriend in Hazlehurst, Georgia, about a two-hour drive east of Albany. He would be gone days at a time from his family. His girlfriend was a cocaine addict, too. He traded cocaine for sex, and she eventually stole Grady's checkbook and wrote a series of bad checks on his account at First State Bank, the same bank he had opened a savings account in when he was in the fifth grade. Like so many times during his period of drug addiction, Grady turned to his mother, Leola, for help. She covered the series of bad checks and cleaned up the financial mess made by the Hazlehurst girlfriend. When Grady fell, and he fell a lot, it was Leola who picked him up and put him back on his feet. He wouldn't stay there long.

After Grady ended his relationship with the Hazlehurst woman, he began to "scheme" up ways to buy drugs. He wasn't working by the late 1980s. He was a fulltime drug addict. He "maxed out credit cards," he said, and at one point got a cash advance on one for $3,000 and bought cocaine. Ten days later, he had smoked the entire amount. He would go through "thousands of dollars" he and Kathleen had saved while he was employed at Albany State. Without telling her until he had done it, Grady refinanced their home and pulled around $25,000 cash out of it.

"I gave Kat $5,000 and I took around $20,000. I used all of that for drugs during that period," Grady said. "At one point back then, I figured I'd probably spent about $100,000 on my drugs. But it was probably more than that in the end."

When the money ran out, Grady had another plan. He proposed an arrangement with his drug suppliers that he would trade them new clothes, computers, almost anything they wanted, that he could steal, for cocaine. They agreed. Grady began shoplifting after some instructions from petty criminals and drug addicts. Grady found a way to feed his habit. The drugs kept coming.

"I shoplifted by order. My major drug dealers told me what they wanted. Clothes, shoes, whatever it was, I got it in exchange for drugs," Grady said. "The shoplifting became another rush. It was easy at first, and I got good at it for a while."

Grady went into the Albany Mall and stole from Gayfers, JC Penney and other stores, sometimes in one day he'd leave with "$1,000 worth of clothes," he said. Sometimes it would be less. It was a childhood friend who showed Grady how to evade store cameras while he was stealing. This worked for a while.

By the time Grady had begun a life of thievery to buy drugs, Kathleen had had enough. She kicked him out of their home during this period, beginning what she called "about a seven-year separation" from Grady. She allowed him to visit the children periodically only when she was certain he was not on drugs during that specific day. There were times when Grady would telephone Kathleen and ask to see the children, but she refused to allow it if she believed "it was a bad time during his drug use. I had to protect my children," Kathleen said. One time when Kathleen was in a drugstore, she saw her husband about to steal some merchandise.

"My mom lived around the corner from Eckerd Drugs on Slappey (Boulevard). I looked at him and he looked awful," Kathleen said. "He had gone from about a 155 pounds to maybe a 125. I gave him some money. I told him, 'Take this and get out of here. You're embarrassing.' "

Grady was living "on the streets some nights" but mostly during this period of separation from Kathleen, before he went to jail and later prison, he lived with his mother. Through his drug addiction Leola always took him in her home, fed him, took care of him, and gave him money. Loretta Travers, Grady's only sibling, moved back to Albany from Chicago by the mid-1980s and began teaching music in the public schools. While away she had spoken with her mother who told her Grady's life was troubled, that he was staying away from his family, partying and drinking and sometimes using drugs.

"When I got back to Albany, I realized it was a lot worse than Momma had told me. I thought he was just doing a lot of partying. Being a party animal," Loretta said. "But he was really into the drugs. I had no doubt he could do anything he wanted with his life. That was the family line he came from. But the drugs had gotten him. His body then was taking so much abuse."

Loretta said she had a conversation with Grady then and told him he was not just hurting himself, but what he was doing was "hurting everybody that loved him." Grady had to "face up to all this love everybody had for him," she said. Loretta told her mother she would have to stop being an enabler, picking Grady up every time he fell and couldn't take care of himself. Eventually that did happen, but it took years.

"Momma really was a big reason he came out of drugs. It was her tenacity. She was a very soft-spoken and caring person," Loretta said. "That was really her legacy. Showing people how to love. But she was also the one who kept him in the drugs" because she covered his debts and took him into her home when Kathleen had kicked Grady out. Love has many sides.

"My mother helped me but she was an enabler. I knew how to pull her strings. I might've recovered sooner," Grady said. "I don't know. It's hard to say. Her enabling stretched my addiction out further than it would've probably gone."

Kathleen reached a point during her separation from Grady that she could do no more. She had suffered enough waiting on Grady to get healthy. She had prayed and cried enough tears to float Grady a long way on a deep river and far out to sea. She held on to her job at Albany State and provided her family with their sole means of financial support as Grady had spent tens of thousands of dollars of their money for his drug habit, including trading it for sex with numerous women. Her faith in Grady had ended, and her faith in God's help was being questioned. At one point, either in the late 1980s or early '90s, Kathleen decided to file for divorce.

She made an appointment to see a local attorney and went into the woman's office, intending to file for divorce. For years the attorney had known and respected Grady's family. Something unexpected happened to Kathleen in that law office that day.

"She said, 'Oh, give him some more time. He's going to be all right. I knew little Grady when he was a boy. He comes from a good family,' I sat there and I didn't know what to do. I remember I got in my car and said to myself, 'What made me walk out of that office?' " Kathleen said.

Through all the years with Grady in and out of jail and prison, Kathleen never attempted again to file for divorce. She loved him. There would be much suffering and many prayers said. But she loved him. "I kept asking God what to do. He never led me to it," Kathleen said.

There were times that together Grady and Kathleen had prayed and asked God to help Grady. Sometime before Grady's first stay in jail for shoplifting, he and Kathleen had met with Rev. E. James Grant of Mt. Zion Baptist Church at his house. They were reaching out for spiritual help. Grady said Rev. Grant told them, 'Just pray and everything will be all right.' I was already praying, but I was still addicted to cocaine."

He quit going to church after that, saying what he was experiencing then at church was "more of a social status than spiritual guidance." During the time he and Kathleen met with Rev. Grant, Grady came to a startling conclusion. He said for the first time he realized he was an addict and his life was being controlled by drugs. "Kathleen and everybody else that cared about me had come to that decision before I did," Grady said. "That was the most frightening experience I ever had in my life. At that moment I realized I could not stop on my own."

The "fear" Grady experienced at that point was unlike anything that had occurred in his life up to that point. For some time he had been thinking his lifestyle with drugs might be one of addiction, but he had yet to fully accept it. "Then I came to the point in my own heart and knew I was addicted," he said. "I had never been defeated by anything in my life, even segregation. I never had something I couldn't overcome, and that includes integration at Albany High and everything I went through there. Knowing I was addicted to drugs was the greatest fear in my life."

Grady stopped attending Mt. Zion Baptist Church, and said he began seeking God on his own. Kathleen and their two youngest children were visiting other churches while Daphne was away at college. Eventually the family began attending New Covenant Church and moved its membership there in 1989. Grady, meanwhile, on his own stopped using drugs for several months and accepted the call to the ministry. This occurred before his shoplifting began. Grady earned an associate degree in theology from Beacon University Christian Life School of Theology in Columbus, Georgia. He had joined New Covenant Church on West Broad Avenue in Albany where Rev. Larry Cornett helped and mentored Grady. Cornett was white and had been one of "the instigators" harassing African American students at Albany High when Grady and Kathleen were there. Cornett had changed. His church was about 30-40 percent African American, Grady said.

Kathleen and the children returned to Mt. Zion Baptist Church in 1998 where Rev. Daniel Simmons had been appointed senior pastor in 1991. Mt. Zion was founded in 1865, the same year the Civil War and slavery ended. Its history in Albany is significant; it includes being the site of mass rallies during the Civil Rights Movement and where Dr. Martin Luther King, Jr. spoke. Since 2010, the church has been located on Westover Boulevard in south Albany and has around 4,000 members, Pastor Simmons said.

He had met both Grady and Kathleen at Albany State when he was a student there in the 1970s. Pastor Simmons was born in Cairo, Georgia, in 1954, about an hour's drive south of Albany. He earned a bachelor's degree in sociology at Albany State and later a master's degree in counseling from the University of Georgia. He was ordained in 1984 and earned a doctorate in the ministry from Bethany Theological Seminary in Dothan, Alabama. By the mid-1980s, as his children and the Caldwells' were attending the same school, Pastor Simmons said he became "close friends" with Grady and Kathleen. When Kathleen returned to Mt. Zion, she became active in helping Pastor Simmons change the church "from traditional to a more contemporary one," he said.

"She (Kathleen) became a valuable asset and ally at Mt. Zion as we made our transition to a more contemporary" church, infusing newer gospel music into the services, Pastor Simmons said. Some members were resistant to change, and Kathleen was able to "reach people that I couldn't."

Pastor Simmons became a counselor to Kathleen and other members of the Caldwell family during this period of Grady's drug addiction. He spent time with Leola Caldwell, Grady's mother, who was a 60-year member of Mt. Zion.

"Any time a person is on drugs, other persons, family members, share the addiction," Pastor Simmons said. "For Leola there was a spiritual, emotional, and physical toll" attributed to the suffering she endured caused by her son's addiction.

Grady did seek Pastor Simmons' counseling during the late 1990s but had not reached the point yet when full restoration would come.

"We would meet, and I'd counsel him. There would be periods where he was away from drugs," but he'd return to them, Pastor Simmons said. "Grady always knew better, but it took him a long time to do better."

When his arrests and time in jail began, Grady said, "I think this is the time God began to deal with me. It would be a long time before I got clean for good. But God was going to deal with me." By the mid-1990s Grady's crime spree in Albany stores had gotten him arrested, and for the next several years he would be in and out of jail in Dougherty County and state prisons, charged with multiple counts of shoplifting, forgery, and violations of probation. Grady never committed an act of violence or carried a weapon when he shoplifted. Throughout the mid- and late-1990s, Grady would get caught, serve time in jail, return to the streets, steal again and return to jail. He was incarcerated in county jails for "about three years, total," he said. He spent several months in state prisons. One document from the Dougherty County Superior Court, signed May 2, 1997, sentenced Grady to jail for eight years, eight months, and nine days, with the possibility of probation after 12 months. God may have been dealing with Grady, but He was in no hurry to fix him.

Other Dougherty County Superior Court documents for Grady from that period include:

- Conviction forgery 1st degree 1996.
- Conviction felony shoplifting 1997.
- Conviction forgery 1st degree 1999.
- Conviction of three cases of felony shoplifting 1999.

There were probation violations as well, and in Lee County Superior Court, just north of Dougherty County, Grady was charged with felony shoplifting 2001.

From jail Grady wrote to Kathleen regularly asking about the children, telling her he wanted forgiveness, and one day, with "God's help" he said he would stop using drugs permanently. Below is a letter from Grady to Kathleen written October 2, 1995, from the Dougherty County Jail. There would be several letters like this to Kathleen.

Dear Kat,

I didn't have the heart to call you because I thought you would have judged me. Though I did mess up once, I was clean when I took the "PISS Test" and should not have been arrested, though God allowed it for a purpose even though He forgave me when I truly repented. Anyway, I am at peace and doing well. I hope you are also.

I must admit I do miss being home and I really miss you. Sometimes I can see your smile, then Satan will try to show me that look of condemnation you can give (smile). It will be interesting to see God work in and through us as a result of all this. When I do get out, I think we should have a serious talk about our desires and intentions. You deserve the best God has for you. If you are in a relationship and want to develop it, I certainly understand, from what I've put you through. I won't hinder you. But if reconciliation is possible, I want to pursue it. That's your call.

I didn't get the money Momma sent me until today, but I owed so many for helping me to this point until it's gone. If you can send a few $, I'd appreciate it. If not, I understand. (Only money orders accepted.) Guess what! I'm not in the kitchen because my weight is good, so God put me in the Commissary. If you need me for any emergency, call here and ask for Commissary. Officer Redding is my boss and he'll let you talk with me.

Oh! I go to court on 10-12-95. We'll see what happens then. If he doesn't release me, I'm thinking about asking him to revoke all my probation so when I get out, my debt will be paid in full. Tell me what you think. I value your opinion.

I talked with Pastor Larry before he left for Russia. I hope he gets my message to come to see me. Give my love to Carmen & Lee (daughter and son). Dap (Daphne), too, if you talk to her. I love you. If God wills, I'll show it soon.

Love,
Grady

Grady was released but not long afterwards he was shoplifting again, was arrested, and sent back to the county jail. In this letter written November 3, 1995, he tried to explain to Kathleen what had happened, what it was that made him steal again.

Dear Kat,

I've really blown it this time. Holy Spirit tried to warn

me of the up-coming attack through you, through scripture, and through my spirit, but I yielded to the attack.

I'm scared of what's going to happen, but I know I brought it on myself. Before I send Momma or you through anything else like this I'd rather die.

I can't describe my thoughts that night. It was as though I was possessed to do it. I tried to put the stuff back, but couldn't. It was as though I had to walk out with it. I never want to experience that feeling again.

Whenever I make it through this, I'll <u>never</u> come back. It's no telling when that will be, I'm facing a felony this time. I'll have a court appointed attorney for the charge, but no representation at my revocation hearing. I pray God touches the heart of some old friend to represent me gratis...

The only consolation I have is that whatever happens, it will not be what I deserve for I've put you, Momma, and the children thru. With God's grace, it will never happen again.

Love,
Grady

It did happen again, several more times. With it always more pain and more prayers to God for help. In the post script to the above letter

Grady asked Kathleen if she could find someone to bring him his Bible. "I need my Bible," he said. He also asked her to let their pastor know he was in jail and if "certain members" wanted to send him money, to do so through money orders. He ended with this: "Satan won this round, but the fight is not over. The victory is mine in Christ."

* * *

Grady wrote this letter from jail to Kathleen November 23, 1995:

Dear Kat,

It's 5:30 pm and we just finished our Thanksgiving Dinner – a bologna sandwich, a salami sandwich, some potato chips and a snack cake. I felt a little depressed this morning. I tried to call and nobody answered. I figured everyone probably went to Atlanta. I really miss being with the family. This is the second year in a row. Well, I have no one to blame but myself. If I can keep that feeling foremost in my mind, I'll never have to worry about going back to drugs again.

I hope at some point during the holiday, you all thought to pray for me. God put it on my heart to pray for everyone, individually, who I thought would be at the Atlanta family gathering. It really lifted my spirits by asking God to bless you all and thanking Him for all of your family and ours.

Lee has really been on my mind. I've been praying for him a lot, so I know he's alright, but tell him to hang in there. It will get better. Did he play any the other night? Tell everyone I love them. I'm figuring you've been too busy to write, and not because you've given up on me.

Love,
Grady

In the letter above Grady was referring to his youngest child, Grady Lee Caldwell III, and only son, known as "Lee." He was an excellent high school basketball and football player and accepted a basketball scholarship to play at Albany State University. In Grady's letters from jail, he always encouraged Kathleen to write him. She did but rarely. Kathleen had all but given up entirely on her husband getting well. Who could question it if she finally did?

"I was just beaten down by then. He'd get out of jail, get caught shoplifting again, and go right back in. I just didn't have much hope that he was ever going to do right again," Kathleen said. "I did visit him once or twice while he was in the Dougherty County Jail and on those occasions his mother asked me to take her there. But I mainly focused on taking care of our children."

Kathleen had a "very close friend" whose husband was incarcerated almost as often as Grady was. Kathleen and the woman talked about their lives and how similar they were with husbands involved in crime and in and out of jail. They had something else in common. The content of the letters they received from their respective husbands was almost identical, Kathleen said. Grady and the friend's husband knew each other well.

In both sets of letters, Kathleen said, their husbands wrote about how they "just knew" God was helping them and hoping their wives would give them "one more chance." The husbands wrote about all the mistakes they had made and all the hurt that they had caused their families. They wrote that when they got out this time, if the wives just take them back, things would be "better forever." Things would finally be well again. Both husbands had learned their lessons, the letters said, and there would be no more crime and drug use.

"The more we talked, we just had to laugh. I told her we could go into business together and sell form letters to inmates," Kathleen said. "When she shared her letters with me, it was like I was reading the ones from Grady. She was like me. It had been hard for both us, but we just had to laugh."

Grady's letters from jail are full of references to God, the Bible, and during at least one stay in jail he organized a Bible study of "about 15-20 people every night and many have been saved and filled with the spirit." There is hopefulness in his tone in almost every letter. He is always seeking Kathleen's love, telling her how strong she is, and how much he still wants to be with her, with God's help. This letter below was dated April 20, 1997.

Dear Kat,

You've been on my mind a lot because I haven't been able to talk with you. Satan was trying to plant all kinds of negative thoughts as to why, but I wouldn't fall for them so he left that alone. I know you're working real hard as well as keeping the family running. Your strength and durability in Christ is phenomenal.

I'm spending a lot of time in the Word. I'm also working through two other books that God is using to help me as well. "The Search For Significance" and "Walking the 12 Steps with Jesus Christ." God is really doing work in me and I'm believing that the manifestation of total deliverance is here. I know deliverance must be maintained and I'm believing He will provide all the needed support for that upon my release.

Last time I talked to Momma she said that you were hosting the prayer group at the house. Tell everybody I said hello, and I'm in good spirits. Thank them for keeping me in their prayers. I go to court May 2nd and please ask whoever will, to stand in agreement with me for God's perfect will to be done by the judge. I'm totally submitting myself to Him, not my will. If I'm not ready to be released, I pray the judge orders me here until God's release date. I have been a reproach to God, you and my family, and the Body of Christ. I'd rather die than continue to treat the Blood of Christ as if it has no effect. I'm through with my will. I'm not ignorant to Satan's devices and I'm tired of being the fool I've been by allowing myself to be caught up in Satan's traps.

I'm ready to walkout my salvation and do what God has for me to do. I pray that you can forgive me and are still willing to walk with me. I do love you, and thank you for everything you've done for the <u>entire</u> family.

Tell Carmen thanks for sending me some money. I told Lee to tell her to send me $50 (just in case I'm not released on May 2) and give you the rest for whatever it's needed for. He told me you got him an Explorer.

I can never make up for all the sacrifices you've had to make because of me, but God's will, I'll show you how much it means to me.

Love,
Grady

Kathleen would continue to sacrifice, suffer, and pray for her lost husband. Grady's problems would not end then, as that letter had hoped they would. He would continue the cycle of release from jail, more drugs, more shoplifting, and violation of probation. Kathleen drew strength from her relationship with God, the love she had for her children, and love and support from friends and family. But Grady's kind of love, if that's what it was, was the killing kind.

"In my mind I would think back then that I was going to get him back the way he once was. But I'd try to get rid of that way of thinking," Kathleen said. "I just got so tired. It was exhausting."

Kathleen talked to her mother, Lois, and sister, Beverly, about whether she ought to divorce Grady and date and maybe eventually remarry. Her mother spoke against divorcing Grady and remarrying, concerned that "another man would be over my children. She was concerned for the safety of my children. My mom never pressured me to divorce," Kathleen said. Grady's relationship with his children, while strained because of what he was allowing drugs to do to him, was never abusive. He was never mean, verbally or physically, to any of their children.

"They loved their father and Grady loved them. We all just wanted him to quit and come home to us and never use drugs again," Kathleen said.

Beverly, who had been arrested as a teenager while participating in civil rights marches in Albany, remembered talking with Kathleen during this period Grady was hooked on drugs and in and out of jail. Beverly herself knew something about strength of character, having been threatened in marches by angry whites, and later enduring days in a crowded jail in Camilla, Georgia. She knew about resolve. What Kathleen had been experiencing for *years* with Grady and her determination to be strong impressed even her sister.

Beverly said she was "angry with Grady" back then and called him "selfish" for what he had done not just to himself, but for how his actions were hurting Kathleen, his children, and others who loved him. Beverly, like so many others, implored Grady to stop the drugs, fix his life, and return to his family and be a *man* again. It had no effect on him. Her anger toward Grady was not eclipsed by the love and concern she had for her sister. She came to admire Kathleen's strength during all of this, more than she ever had in the past.

"I don't know what carried her through those times. I asked her about all the embarrassment. And I knew it was hard for her," Beverly said. "Grady was a smart guy, very smart. He was a great speaker. But Kat didn't miss a beat. She kept going, held her head up. She was amazing. And I was amazed back then by how she could stay so focused with her job and her children. She even looked so radiant back then."

At one point Beverly tried to convince her sister to divorce Grady, and that their marriage wasn't going to survive, things were "not going to work out." Grady was never going to get better. Beverly said she thought then that once a drug addict, always a drug addict. Kathleen did not give up. "Kathleen would just say, 'We just got to pray for Grady,'" Beverly said. The prayers were not yet working in full. The prayers never stopped.

"Kathleen never, *never* called me crying and complaining. There was never a sense that, 'Woe unto me!' She wasn't a complainer. I still don't know how she did it," Beverly said.

Dr. C. W. Grant, who hired both Kathleen and Grady to work at Albany State, said Grady survived through God's will and through the love of Kathleen. Even "God ought to have been scared" knowing what Grady had put himself through: The drugs, the corrupt sexual behavior, and the life of crime. "Wherever God had to go to get Grady" in the end, it was an awful, evil, dark place. God's deliverer was Kathleen, he said.

"She's been a great source of strength and had every right to leave him and didn't. No one would've blamed her," Grant said. "But God put Kathleen there. She never, never violated her marriage vows. I would've known it. She simply was very strong. She has her own integrity."

Grady emotionally "wrecked" his mother and Kathleen for years, Grant said. Both were strong women who Grady learned from in the end.

"It was through Kat I learned how to love. I had been so self-centered in my life. Everything was about me. She and my mother taught me how to love," Grady said. "I don't know how she did it. Once she even drove me to the home of another woman, who I had been sleeping with, so I could pick up some bounced checks. I put Kat through so much."

In a three-page letter from the Coastal State Prison in Garden City, Georgia, dated September 5, 1997, Grady refers to his self-centered life. He had been transferred there from the Dougherty County Jail Facility. The pain he was causing others seemed it would never stop.

Dear Kat,

This is the first time I've been in a position to write you back since I was transferred from D.C.J. F. I got your letter on the day they moved me to Coastal. I was in a deep sleep that night when they woke me up about 2:00 am and told me to "roll-it-up." There are only two reasons they tell you to "roll-it-up"-either you are going to be transferred to prison or you're being moved for disciplinary reasons. I just knew neither of those could be the case. So I thought God had done me like he did Peter when all the prison doors were opened and he went home (smile). But it was too early in the morning for that (smile). Then reality set in when the officer told me in a language I could not help but understand, I was being shipped.

One thing for sure, this is not the Whitehouse nor is it a place for performing on stage. This place makes D. C.

J. look like a resort. Maybe not quite that bad but there's a considerable difference. So if you are not able to see whatever you are looking for in me once I get out of here, I guess it will never be seen. I guess it will just not be in me.

Daphne was right about one thing she told me after visiting me at the YDC (Grady had been sent on a work detail at the Youth Development Center in Albany). I don't ever recall being as nervous and scared as I was when she pulled up. She didn't come at the time she had said and I was feeling disappointed and the enemy was beating up on me, planting thoughts that she didn't want to see me and didn't love me anymore from all the hurt and pain I've caused you, mostly, as well as everyone else in my life. I was surprised when she did come, I could hardly talk to her about anything, not to mention what I had planned on talking to her about. That's why I had to call her when I got the chance and talk to her. So she was right, I was not myself when she saw me. I don't fully understand it myself, but that's the best I can explain.

Kat, I can't blame you for not ever wanting us back together. You deserved so much more than the pain I've caused. At least now I know how you feel – I guess you were saying you no longer want to be my wife, or God has His work cut out for Him to put us back together.

I've hurt you so badly I'd rather die than put you through all the things I've done. The fear of failing you again is too overwhelming for me. I feel the same way about what I've put Momma through. I didn't understand what you meant about when you told me about Momma being sick – I guess I am just that self-centered or clueless. Maybe I need to just leave Albany and get away from everybody I love so I won't kill you all with my love. I pray God will reveal the answers I need to know. I know I can't listen to what I think.

I prayed to God to allow me to eat Thanksgiving dinner with the family once again. I believe that's why he allowed me to come here – to put me in position for that prayer to be answered. That will be worth everything I'm going through. More than that, I want His will to be done in both of our lives.

Either way it goes, I pray God will heal all the hurt I've caused you. I want what's best for you to be done more than what I want to be done. You deserve it.

Love,
Grady

P.S. Keep me in your prayers. I do love you and would like to show my love.

* * *

In the folder of letters Grady gave me that he had written to Kathleen, most when he was in jail and prison during his years away from his family, there was something that immediately grabbed my attention. It was a brightly colored, red, purple, and green handmade valentine card to Kathleen. At the bottom it was signed by "Sherman." Grady doesn't remember where he was, who Sherman was, or the year it was drawn. He does remember that he had it drawn special for Kat. "It was a valentine card for her. I just can't recall the other details about it," Grady said. "It is beautiful though."

There is a red rose drawn in the middle of the eight-by-ten lineless, white paper. Next to the rose with a green stem are two Bible verses. One is from the New Testament, the book of John: *Let not your heart be troubled: Ye believe in God, believe also in me.*

The second one is from the Old Testament, the book of Proverbs: *Trust in the Lord with all thy heart and lean not unto thy own understanding. In all thy ways acknowledge Him and He shall direct thy paths.*

Below the verses there are two purple hearts intertwined. One reads "Grady" and the other "Kat." Below the heart, at the bottom of the page, this is written:

You are the beautiful rose of my life. You are my tomorrow and yesterday. You are my thoughts of a good wife; you are why I always pray God, Let your light shine on me, make it for the whole world to see. You were sent from heaven above, to share with me all your love.

Grady told me several times over our many interviews he eventually would learn how to love through Kathleen, but it would take a long, long time. With love there is always suffering. The deeper the love, so it is with the suffering. She wrote him a few letters during the years he was in rehab and jail, though not as many as he wrote her. Grady could find none of those letters today. He had lost them over the years as he had lost so many things.

EIGHT

"I think one of the things that we can learn from Grady's story is that there is a God. No man could've brought Grady back," Grant said. "If a man could've, I could've done it. I tried. Grady couldn't save himself because he is a man."

If what Grant said is true, then it was God doing His work after Grady was finally sentenced for 18 months in the late 1990s to the Jefferson County Correctional Institute in Louisville, Georgia, a three-hour drive north of Albany, after a series of probation violations, continual drug use, shoplifting and forgery convictions.

William Evans was the warden of the Jefferson Correctional Institute when Grady was sentenced there, and in 2012 Evans was still working in that capacity. Many of Evans' prisoners were assigned to work details like clearing brush, cutting grass, and doing other physical work outside of the prison. Because Grady was a little older than most of the inmates, Evans assigned Grady to work inside the prison. Grady became an orderly for one of the dorms that included 22 other inmates. Evans gave him responsibility. Grady did not disappoint him. "He did an excellent job for me. He made sure the dorms were cleaned, that the inmates got their laundry and any information that they needed. Those other inmates respected him," Evans said.

As he had done while in jail in Albany, at Louisville Grady continued to read the Bible, pray, conduct Bible sessions, and provide counseling to help fellow inmates. Each day he thought of Kathleen. He wrote her letters and phoned her when he could. Her responses were sporadic. No one could blame her. Whatever hope she had had over this long period of her husband getting well, by the time Grady was sentenced to Louisville, it had all but disappeared, much like the man Grady once was.

Warden Evans said it was "beneficial to let these other guys" hear Grady's counseling and life story. Grady seemed intent on finally changing, and he was trying to help others like himself. This time it was going to be different.

"He could talk from a different perspective than other counselors could. He had been locked up before I got him. His message could really reach home to some of these guys," Evans said. "He became a model inmate for me. He led so many church activities, and he had a beautiful singing voice. He was just very respectful."

"There came a point for me under Warden Evans, and he was good to me, where I made up my mind to get clean," Grady said. "God was finally working through me. I know it now. I felt it when it was happening."

"The whole time Grady was up in Louisville I was still thinking he'd probably never get well," Kathleen said. "I had all but given up. God did begin to work through Grady."

Grady's release from the Jefferson Correctional Institute in 2001 did not end his connection with Warden Evans and that prison. "I am still in contact with Grady. Once a year he normally comes through here to speak with our inmates," Evans said. "He'll counsel them. He's going to do it this year (2011). He's a fine individual. I have a lot of respect for him."

When Grady was finally released from the prison in Louisville, Georgia, he asked Kathleen if he could come back home, start again and this time make everything better. She refused. This had been the way it was many times before, and Grady would eventually return to drugs and crime. She would not let him come home to Albany to be with her. Grady did not give up.

He was living in Albany with is mother in 2001 and was troubled that Kathleen would not accept him back into her home. "Kat and I had a spat. I was upset she didn't take me back," Grady said. Once again he began using drugs and shoplifting to buy them. He stole merchandise from Wal-Mart in Lee County. Grady admitted himself to a residential drug rehabilitation clinic in Hampton, Georgia, just south of Atlanta. This was the beginning of his full recovery. It was called Soul Changers Recovery Program Inc., a non-profit organization co-founded by Jimmy Moss in the early 1990s. Moss said he was the chief executive officer of the "spiritual-based" treatment program when Grady arrived. Grady spent about a year in the program, living in a duplex, working in an area warehouse during the day. During the evenings and weekends, he attended counseling sessions and church service at the instruction of Soul Changers. Moss had seen hundreds of "clients" like Grady who had almost killed themselves with drug and alcohol abuse while causing great sorrow within their families. He noticed from the beginning Grady was intent on changing his life.

"I remember when Grady first came in to us he was so downtrodden spiritually. But he got right to work with rebuilding his relationship with

God," Moss said. "Number one you got to change your mind, then your actions, and your lifestyle will eventually change. Through the grace of God, Grady did all that. After a period with us, he was beginning to finally change his life for the better."

There had been other rehabs, years both in jail and in prison and on probation, but it was during his time at Soul Changers where Grady said he had been filled with God's strength and was able to overcome the seductive lure of cocaine. Finally, he would defeat it. Grady's evenings were filled with prayer, Bible study, and church on the weekends. He was finding peace that had eluded him for many years. It was the rebirth for which he had longed, hoped, and prayed. It wasn't too late, he thought to himself during that time at Soul Changers, to properly love Kathleen, his children, family and friends. It must never be too late to love in full. Much had been lost, but he was seeking authentic redemption by this period. Much could be gained.

"Like I was when I came out of prison, when I went to Soul Changers, I had finally made up my mind to get clean and stay clean. God was helping me," Grady said. "At the same time I stopped trying to put my relationship back with Kat. We were communicating, but I wasn't pressuring her. I was praying to God to restore my marriage."

All the while Kathleen was very cautious. She had for many years heard him "promise" he was going to be better if she would just give him "one more chance." He said it each time after finishing a stay in a rehabilitation clinic and after being released from prison. He said it a hundred times in his letters. She had heard it all so many times before. "At first I didn't think it (Soul Changers) was going to be any different" than his other attempts at rehabilitation, she said. As the months went by, however, she began to see something different happening within her husband.

"He had been there about a year before I could see brokenness in him," Kathleen said. "He had finally become dependent on the Lord. Grady was not puffed up anymore. I saw the brokenness myself. At Soul Changers he totally surrendered to God."

Grady used the Greek word "kairos" to describe what happened to him at Soul Changers. While Greek is the original language of the New Testament, kairos is translated as the "right or opportune moment."

"This was God's appointed time in dealing with me. It was His season. I had asked for the healing through much prayer and meditation" while at Soul Changers, Grady said.

Kathleen said after Grady completed the program at Soul Changers, God was telling her this time was different. Authentic healing within her husband was occurring. "The other times he went into rehabs - going back and forth - when he got out, I always had fear he'd go back again," Kathleen said. "After Soul Changers, I never had that fear again."

When Grady completed "one clean year" at Soul Changers, Moss asked him to volunteer to serve on the board of directors and help others who had fallen like Grady but wanted to be back again standing strong. Grady accepted the position. He met with many clients, telling them about his life story in the hopes that they would see the "hope and you can defeat drugs and alcohol," Grady said.

"I counseled addicts at Soul Changers the same way I talked with inmates in prison. I know what they are feeling," Grady said. "I know that if they are determined and allow God to work through them, they can whip drugs. They can regain their lives."

After a year or so working at Soul Changers, Grady joined the ministerial staff at Zion Baptist Church in Hampton, Georgia, under Rev. Nathaniel Lee. On September 28, 2003, he was ordained by Lee, and it was an event Grady recognized as "one of the first stages of God's restoration. I realized then God would still use me after the things I've gone through." He became assistant pastor under Lee. Included at the ordination were Kathleen, all of their children, his close friends Dr. James Woods and his wife Ella, and former classmates. "My mother and sister came, too," Grady said. "That was big for me to have my mother with me. God had given me a promise that my mother would see me clean and walking in God's purpose for my life before she passed. He fulfilled that promise, praise the Lord!"

About this time he asked Kathleen if he could attend a family reunion with her. The reunion was in Virginia and organized by Al Walden's family, who was married to Kathleen's sister, Beverly. Grady was now applying a "little pressure" to Kathleen, hoping she would take him with her. He was hoping God would see this through. He had prayed and prayed for it.

Grady during the same year had been ordered by the court to return to South Georgia and face shoplifting charges from 2001 when he stole from the Lee County Wal-Mart. The case had been backlogged, which turned out to be an advantage for Grady. "Had they heard my case after I shoplifted, they might've sent me to prison for 10 years," Grady said.

When he appeared before the court for the last time in 2003, he had been drug free for around two years and working in the ministry. The judge allowed him to return to Hampton and continue in the ministry. Grady did that while trying to restore his marriage with Kathleen.

"Grady kept telling me 'God has a plan for us to get back together.' But I had heard things like that many times," Kathleen said. "He had been, as far as I could tell, clean from drugs for a few years by then. But I still wasn't certain."

She had other concerns. For about six months before the scheduled family reunion, Kathleen had been dating someone she had known when she was attending Albany State College. He was living in Tennessee, was divorced, and had been spending time with Kathleen. He wanted to go to the family reunion with her, Kathleen said.

"I thought and prayed about what to do. He wanted to go, and he wanted our relationship to grow," Kathleen said. "I realized, though, that I wasn't ready to get intimate with him. So I told him no, and then I let Grady go with me."

"I felt like when she said 'yes' I just knew God was going to make this work. *Finally*. I had been clean for a few years, and I was going to stay that way," Grady said. "We had fun at the reunion. God had worked through me. It just took Him a while."

Since that family reunion, Grady and Kathleen have been together. For the next few years Kathleen maintained their home in Albany, Grady lived in an apartment in Hampton, Georgia, working with the Zion Baptist Church. She would later join Grady in Hampton.

Grady came out of the Jefferson County Correctional Institute determined to stay clean. While he was still there, he was visited by his daughter Yolanda Graham, who had been born out of wedlock in 1966 to Grady and Annie Kate Graham. This was the child that Grady had abandoned, and only a couple of times since her birth had he taken the time to see her. Inside of her were longstanding feelings of hurt, anger, and frustration directed toward the father she never knew. Grady's road to redemption would include reconciliation with many he had hurt. He needed God's strength to do so.

"I did visit him at Louisville (Jefferson County Correctional Institute). I actually went with my newly-connected sister, Daphne. The trip allowed us an opportunity to bond and to get to know each other. It was all kind of surreal. At that point I wanted to let bygones be bygones. We (Yolanda and Grady) had traded letters during that period. But I wasn't ready for a relationship," Yolanda said. "He was trying to apologize for everything that had happened. After that visit in prison, I started developing some understanding and empathy for him. I remember having some sense of contentment when I left."

That sense of contentment took decades for Yolanda to realize. She didn't learn Grady was her father until she was about "eight or nine," and she was living in Albany with her great-aunt after her mother had moved out of town. She was watching the local evening news with a cousin when Grady's picture appeared because he was involved in local political activities during that time.

"I was somewhat dumbfounded when my cousin told me Grady was my father. The ironic thing is back then my grandmother, Leola (Grady's mother), was teaching at my elementary school," Yolanda said.

It would be a few years after that before Grady decided to see his daughter. He said he, Kathleen, and even his mother for years all agreed to deny paternity. Later they would all regret their decisions. Grady's first contact with Yolanda was when she was about 13. He telephoned Yolanda's house, spoke to her aunt Ella Graham, and arranged a meeting between them. Grady said he wanted to reach out to her, but neither he nor Kathleen were ready to embrace Yolanda as part of their family.

"He came over to visit and came in my living room. I guess it wasn't unnatural or unheard of not to know your father. But I was hurt. I had been hurt," Yolanda said. "We went out to lunch and found out we had some common interests like martial arts. I remember that being kind of fascinating. Shortly after that he disappeared and I never heard from him again."

Not long after Grady's visit, Yolanda moved with family to New Jersey, and during this period she wrote Grady a few letters, but he didn't return any. After high school, she enrolled at Cornell University in Ithaca, New York, and was pre-med and majoring in human development and family studies. She had all but given up on having a relationship with her father. Then in December of 1985 she received a telephone call from him. He called around December 14 or 15 to wish her a happy birthday, she said. Her birthday is December 21.

"I was angry and told him that it wasn't my birthday. He started telling me about his addiction to drugs, even doing heroin, and that he had been incarcerated," Yolanda said. "I said 'Fine, have a good time, I don't want any part of that.' He was very apologetic and wanted to have a relationship. I was just so hurt by that phone call. I wasn't receptive."

Yolanda graduated from Cornell, and then earned her M.D. at the State University of New York at Buffalo in 1992. From there she returned to Georgia and trained at Emory University in Atlanta where she specialized in child and adolescent psychiatry. For the past several years she has been practicing medicine in the Atlanta area. By the summer of 2011, she was the medical director at Devereux Georgia Treatment Network in Kennesaw. There she works with children who, like herself, experienced periods of trauma, neglect, and pain because of the actions of adults in their lives. They need healing.

Her decision to practice psychiatry was influenced by her own family struggles and the sense of loss and pain she experienced as a child. She didn't realize it in the beginning but came to understand it as she moved from undergraduate to medical school. Both love and pain can influence chosen paths.

"What happened to me as a child I'm sure had a lot to do with my career choice. I didn't know it at the time," Yolanda said. "I deal with children every day who think I have no understanding of their problems. That's interesting because I do. I know exactly what they're going through."

About the time Yolanda visited Grady in the state prison in Louisville, Georgia, she decided to reach out to her grandmother, Leola Caldwell. By the late 1990s, Yolanda had contacted Leola and began making the three-hour drive from Atlanta south to Albany to visit her. The visits went well. Leola welcomed her grandchild in ways she had not done when Yolanda was younger, a time when "she was telling Grady to deny paternity. She seemed sorry for what she did back then," Yolanda said.

After a few visits with Leola, they agreed it was time for Yolanda to meet the rest of the family. Grady was in and out of jail during this period, still addicted to drugs, but he and Kat agreed to see Yolanda at their home. The visit did not reconcile daughter and father. When the visit finally occurred, Grady was incarcerated again.

"It was a strange experience. My partner, Tiffany Courtney-Graham, went with me and we didn't stay very long, and we didn't resolve anything," Yolanda said. It was the first time Yolanda and her siblings had come "face to face. I didn't keep contact with them after that, but I continued to see Leola. I even went to her funeral. I remained close with her until she passed."

It was sometime after Yolanda visited Grady in prison and he had been released when the two would inadvertently come in contact again. When Grady began undergoing treatment for his addiction south of Atlanta their paths crossed through mutual friends. She was angered by the fact he had told others that he was her father.

"I didn't like hearing that. He was part of my genetic makeup. I didn't consider him my father. Not the way I had been neglected all those years," Yolanda said. But the two did begin to talk during that period and spend time together. "We started working on a relationship."

Grady had changed and now finally he appeared to be free from drugs. He was trying to rebuild fractured relationships, long fractured by his selfish drug addiction. That included rebuilding them with Kathleen and all of his children. Kathleen had changed too, Yolanda said. She began to welcome Yolanda into her family. It would be a few years before Yolanda would be able call Grady "*my dad or my father,*" but it would happen. God was working through all of them. They all said it was so.

"That was a huge transition for me. At that point he had been clean for about eight years," Yolanda said.

Leola arranged for all of her grandchildren to inherit some money from her after her death. That included Yolanda. "We are close now and it feels like a family," Yolanda said. "There's no way to erase the past but we haven't let it stop us from building a future."

Yolanda does not give herself or Grady credit for what happened several years ago during the beginning of this reconciliation process that has enriched both of their lives. It was Kathleen who encouraged the two to develop a family relationship. And it was Kathleen who had to change herself before she began to accept Yolanda as part of her family. "Kathleen was amazing. If it wasn't for her, this thing would've never happened," Yolanda said. "She apologized for her decisions in the past, and I forgave her."

"I was wrong back then. I asked God to forgive me, and I asked Yolanda to forgive me. She's part of our family now," Kathleen said. "That's the way it should be. When we have family gatherings, Yolanda is with us, and she always will be." That includes Yolanda's partner of 15 years, Tiffany Courtney-Graham, and their two children, Meghann and Grayson.

For Grady, now looking back on his own behavior when he neglected Yolanda, he regrets his initial denial of paternity and all of the years in which he failed to be a father to her. It was "selfish of me" to have acted in that way, Grady said. The road to redemption can take many years. Grady said he apologized to all of his children and to Kathleen many times for the pain and disappointment he caused for so long.

"Yolanda forgave me for what I didn't do all those years," Grady said. "She is a strong and loving person to have done that. I wasn't a father to her. I can't go back and fix that, but she's part of our family now."

Of Yolanda's relationship with her partner, Tiffany, Grady said: "Even though I totally disagree with her lifestyle in a same sex relationship, it does not change my love for her, or for Tiffany whom I have grown to love.

"I believe the Word of God is clear about same sex relationships and God does not change based on today's world view. He is the same yesterday, today, and forever. We have talked about it and she knows how I feel and I know how she feels. I thought that by me not being the father that I should have been may have had an effect on her sexuality. However, she assured me that it had little, if anything to do with it.

"Neither of us will allow our differences over that issue to hinder our relationship or love for each other. One thing is for sure, each one of us has to stand before God and give an account of ourselves."

NINE

Kathleen found strength through prayer, family, and friends who helped her during Grady's many years of addiction and incarceration. One couple in particular was Dr. James Woods and his wife Ella who moved to Albany in the mid-1970s and a short time later met Grady and Kathleen as all four were attending New Covenant Church. The church later moved from Washington Street to Broad Avenue, but the relationship that was formed between the couples stayed strong, growing over the years when Grady was suffering and so was Kathleen. Woods was introduced to Kathleen and Grady by one of his patients who worked with her at Albany State College. What Kathleen didn't know then was how much she would come to rely on Woods when the troubles began.

Woods was an obstetrician and gynecologist and was born in Norfolk, Virginia, in 1943. He came to Albany in 1976 to practice medicine at the behest of Dr. Willie Adams. The two had been classmates at Meharry Medical College in Nashville, Tennessee. By the early 2000, Adams would be elected the first African American mayor of Albany. Woods had served in the Navy and completed his residency at Oakland Naval Hospital in California. He had "no intentions of coming to Georgia" to practice medicine until Adams asked him to join his practice. Woods said he has been working in Albany ever since, and after meeting

Grady and Kathleen, he and his wife developed a "strong friendship" with the Caldwells that endures today.

"All of us just happened to like each other. It's been that way ever since," Ella said. She is from Birmingham, Alabama, and they have been married for 45 years. They had three boys they've reared together, all in Christian love.

By the early 1980s, the couples were socializing together and Kathleen had become one of Woods' patients. They had fun together. A strong bond was forming among the four of them. Woods took an immediate liking of Grady, describing him as a man who would accomplish many good things in his life. He said Grady was a "smart and gifted man" and a good singer, too.

"They were Christians and we all had the same beliefs. We started a group with some other church members called 'Bread Breakers.' It was a fellowship meeting for couples," Woods said. "We rotated from house to house. We had dinner together and talked about our faith."

At these gatherings discussions developed about how to live a Christian life, the importance of family love, and having a relationship with Jesus Christ. There were Bible readings. They served food and talked casually about family, jobs, and personal aspirations. They all said it was a good time. Grady was there in the beginning speaking about the Bible, family, and Christian love. He and Kathleen hosted the group at their house, enjoying the sense of community and Christian spirit. Kathleen continued to host the group when Grady's behavior changed and she would not allow him to live with her and their children. Sometimes Kathleen hosted the group and Grady was in jail writing letters to Kathleen asking for her and God to forgive him. Bread Breakers continued meeting without Grady. The Woods never visited Grady when he was in jail and later prison, a time when Kathleen turned to them for guidance.

Ella said it was an encounter with Grady at church sometime in the early or mid-1980s when she realized the seriousness of his drug problems. Grady wanted money from her to buy drugs. "I remember one time, and this was when it hit me about his addiction, Grady said, 'Can I borrow 20 dollars?' I said no," Ella said. "Then he said, 'How about 15?' I still said no. He went to ten and then five, and I still said no. I knew what he wanted the money for."

By that period Kathleen knew painfully well how expensive Grady's addiction had become. It was the same period she was relying heavily on the friendship of James and Ella Woods. "He and Ella were good to me during that whole period. They stood by me all those years. They didn't judge me," Kathleen said. "They showed true Christian love. Their friendship meant a lot to me. It still does."

Woods said he "liked Grady as a person" and when he realized Grady was a drug addict, the pain he was causing Kathleen and others who loved him, he didn't dwell on it. Instead he tried to develop a "commitment" within to help Kathleen. Christians should seek not to judge but to help, Woods said.

"I had been very fortunate to have had the opportunity to talk to Kathleen when she was overwhelmed," Woods said. "What Grady was doing never impacted my friendship with him or her. There were times when she was about to give up the ship."

Kathleen and Woods talked, prayed together, and asked God for help many times instead of allowing the ship to go down with her husband. Woods said he never "criticized Grady" but in his counseling sessions with Kathleen, he tried to focus on saying and doing things that would give her "spiritual strength." He kept faith in her and faith in God.

"She is a strong woman. Very strong. They probably talked more back then than Kathleen and I did," Ella said.

"What can you say except she exemplifies a strong woman with strong principles. We prayed together a lot about the problem. She's really just a beautiful individual," James Woods said.

There were other things Woods could say and did say about the strength of Kathleen, a theme consistent with everyone I interviewed who was close to her as she found the resiliency, with God's guidance, needed to endure what her husband was putting her through all those years. Woods said it took an exceptional person to stay by Grady, forgive him, and work to rebuild their relationship and family. Love can be powerful. God is powerful. When Grady got out of prison and began his rehabilitation with Soul Changers in Hampton, Georgia, Woods went to visit him and what he saw in Grady was a "spiritual shift" with the promise of healing and full redemption. The shift continues today. "I'd like to think the underlying basis of all of this is Godly love," Woods said.

Today when Grady and Kathleen leave their home near Griffin, Georgia, to visit family and friends in Albany, they usually spend the nights with the Woods, who live in a ranch-style home on Wexford Drive. Woods continues to practice medicine in Albany, and as of 2011 he was working for Albany Area Primary Health Care. His clinic was at 401 South Madison Street. When Grady came to Albany in June of 2011 for the Fiftieth Anniversary of the Albany Civil Rights Movement and to visit old friends like Gil Anderson, Grady spent a few nights with James and Ella Woods. Grady said it was a feeling of comfort for him to be with old friends who helped Kathleen and him years ago, old friends who provided guidance as they "walked in and lived the Word of God." That helps sustain Grady even now as he has been drug-free for more than eleven years.

"I was just blessed to have friends like Dr. Woods and Ella. God worked through them to help me and Kathleen," Grady said. "We're all close. They didn't give up on me, and they gave Kat so much spiritual counseling. We'll be close for a long time."

For Woods, his friendship with Grady and Kathleen has been longstanding, providing help when Grady's addiction became apparent.

"That's what Christianity is supposed to be about. Love and helping one another. Our friendship has grown even closer the past few years," Woods said. "When he sees me now, Grady calls me, 'Rev. Dr. Daddy.' I kind of like that. We have great exchanges every time we get together."

Parts of the two letters below indicate the closeness between Woods and Grady. Both were written when Grady was in the Dougherty County Jail. Grady wrote the first one June 6, 1996, and the other on July 13, 1996.

Dear Rev. Dr. Daddy,

Just bringing you up to date. I understand that my release date will be around July 31. I feel in my spirit I'll be out before then, to the glory of God. I was hoping to have gotten out by the first week in June. One thing I've learned, not my will but His. He knows the exact date He wants me out and no demon in hell can keep me any longer. Until then I rest in His will and do what he has me doing in here...

Thanks for keeping me and my family in your prayers. Tell Ella I said hello.

Your son in Christ,
Grady

Dear Rev. Dr. Daddy,

I pray this letter finds you and yours in good health and spirit. I just wanted to touch base and let you know things here are fine. Jesus is still Lord! The Bible study group is going strong every night and God has been doing a mighty work.

I feel in my spirit that the Lord may release me next week. He has developed the Bible study to the point that when I leave, it will continue. He just moved a couple of brothers in this unit who are able to continue. It's amazing to see God move. Oh!

The Lord had put in my heart to start a support group for X-inmates. Since I've been here, I've seen so many brothers return over and over again. This has been a revolving door. Sin has a way of doing that doesn't it? I'll tell you more about it when I see you. I'm mad with the enemy and ready to take back what he's stolen from me and my family.

Keep me in your prayers as you are in mine.

In Christ,
Grady

TEN

In January 2011, Kathleen and Grady came to Albany from their home near Griffin, Georgia, and I interviewed both of them during that period while the three of us drove through their old neighborhood where they grew up, met, and later fell in love. I saw Kathleen's family home, and Grady said he first kissed her while they were standing on the wooden front porch. He pointed to it, smiled and looked at her when he told me the story. She smiled back at him. Not far from her home we drove by Gil Anderson's house on Cedar Avenue, Grady's best friend. Gil's father was Dr. William Anderson, local civil rights leader and overnight host to Dr. Martin Luther King, Jr. when he came to town to lead marches for civil rights in the early 1960s. In that house Grady got to know Dr. King, one the world's most noted figures of the 20th century and winner of the Nobel Peace Prize in 1964. Grady and Kathleen shared many good memories with me of their families, friends, and coming of age back then. They reminded me how difficult and sometimes dangerous it could be for them simply because they were African Americans. They were strong then and had to be.

During their stay in Albany, Grady was part of a panel discussion at the Albany Civil Rights Institute joining three other African Americans who, like himself, graduated from the historically all-white Albany High School in 1967. The program was titled: Back to School/Integration

101. An overflow crowd of around a hundred filled the meeting room at the Institute to hear the four activists tell their stories. Including Grady there was Mary Jones Wright, Robert D. Thomas, and Patricia Chatmon Perryman. Grady seemed relaxed and confident that night speaking forcefully about his experience in the school and being the first African American to integrate the football team. Patricia's father was Thomas C. Chatmon, Sr., a civil rights leader in Albany. That night, January 27, 2011, she said, "Every day was a battlefield" describing the racist attitudes among many white students when the foursome were enrolled there. The other three agreed.

Dr. Lee Formwalt, then the executive director of the Albany Civil Rights Institute, provided more historic perspective of what Grady and his classmates had endured back then.

"Many white adults in the 1960s resented the Civil Rights Movement, which was really an attack on their white privilege," he said. "Their high school children shared some of their attitudes, which made it very difficult for African American students who were perceived as outsiders at the historically white school."

A year later Grady was invited back to Albany for a much bigger event having accepted an invitation as keynote speaker at the King Celebration 2012. City leaders for years have organized the event to promote the life and work of Dr. King and his connection to Albany. Hundreds of people attend each year at the James H. Gray, Sr. Civic Center downtown Albany, not far from where Dr. King led marches and was arrested in the early 1960s. Now Grady, having with the help of God restored his life to decency and respect, had been asked to come and tell his story. Kathleen would be by his side.

Grady was introduced January 16, 2012, by Greg Fullerton, a local white attorney and a classmate of his when they both attended Albany High in the mid-1960s. He spoke for a few minutes about Grady's life and called him a star on the school football team during "challenging times for our community as we sought to unite black and white communities, not only in sports and education but in our politics, our economics, our neighborhoods and our children's futures." Fullerton had recognized then the leadership potential within Grady. Many other whites would've been too embittered to do so during that decade.

Fullerton called his "friend and native son" a man of respect and dignity during those early years and helped Albany change for the better breaking racial barriers at Albany High.

"Like Dr. Martin Luther King, Jr., the young Grady Caldwell in his own way, with his own God-given talents was the symbolic but very effective force for that change. I remember that he always held his head up high with a cheerful, determined spirit to preserve whether on the football field or off. That took courage to see those small, brave steps in the right direction of what changed the world," Fullerton said.

Putting Grady's story in world-context is where it should be. The most successful social and political movement in the 20th century may well have been the modern American Civil Rights Movement. Many played a role and risked their lives. So did Grady Lee Caldwell, Jr.

Then Grady came to the podium dressed sharply in a suit and tie, and Kathleen, with a flower pinned to her dress, was sitting at the table along the stage next to him. She looked up at him as he began. Kat was next to the podium, always Kat by his side. He spoke forcefully, rhythmically, and in a manner reminiscent of great orators. Rev. Grady Caldwell is a powerful public speaker. He began not in prose but in poetry.

"I dreamed many dreams that never came true... I have realized enough of my dreams - thank God - that makes me keep dreaming...I prayed many prayers when no answer came. I've waited patient long but answers have come to enough of my prayers to make me keep praying on..." He went on like this for a few moments and then began speaking of his own journey, the awful mistakes he made, and the redemptive powers of God. The speech was beautiful in its cadence. Grady's speaking style, the way he uses language, reminded me of films I've seen of Dr. King's speeches in the 1960s. He is that good. There were young and old in the audience, African American and white. Many I'm sure not fully aware of Grady's years of crime and drug addiction. Those were painful years for his family and others who knew him well.

"Those of you who *really* know me, you know only by the grace of God and mercy of God that I stand before you today...I'm a living testimony for the God I serve is a God of restoration...If God can use me with everything I've gone through there's nobody in this room, nor listening on television that has any excuse of why God can't or won't use you. I believe that understanding is the best thing in the world," Grady said.

He began listing several names out of Albany's past, of teachers, preachers, and mentors, leaders all who helped guide him, believed in him, all stressing the value of a formal education. They helped form his early character. He ended this list with his mother. "I see Leola Caldwell – my mother – the personification of unconditional love. I tell you it's mighty crowded up here," Grady said.

What Grady didn't say was that in the 1990s he was arrested on forgery charges for stealing, signing, and cashing his mother's checks. Few in the crowd probably knew of that.

He listed adults who helped him when he was a child including his "surrogate father," Dr. William Anderson, president of the Albany Movement, the local civil rights organization in the 1960s. From there Grady's story covered his football days and being the "first Negro at Albany High and one of only three in the state" who integrated white teams at that time. He spoke directly about his life and the years wasted with drugs and selfish behavior. And he spoke about the work of God, His work through Grady's own life.

But how does one go from a pioneer in sports to a professional career, to politics in the city, to the pit of prison and of addiction, to the purpose and plans of God? For I am a testimony of the redemptive power of God.

While we are here to celebrate the birthday of Dr. Martin Luther King, Jr., we are really here to celebrate what God accomplished through a vessel that was surrendered to God's purpose for his life. And Dr. King's willingness for his potential to be maximized by following the purpose and plans of God.

My Bible says only a fool would say in his heart that there is no God. Scientists have proven man only uses 10-12 percent of his mental capacity. Let's give us 15 percent. That means there's 85 percent of stuff out there to be known that's not known. God knows everything. Oh, let me say that again: *God knows everything.* If we as a nation are not careful, greed and self-centeredness are going to cause us to self-destruct. Everybody's focused on me, myself, and I; the unholy trinity.

You see it's really not about you and it's really not about me. It's about how God wants to use each one of us to impact someone else's life. Just like he used Dr. King. We must do a critical self-examination. Am I doing anything that will directly impact the life of someone else for the better without me receiving any personal gain? Or am I engaged in many lesser things that may satisfy my personal conscience and gratify my desire to do something without getting outside my comfort zone?"

Then his message turned to national politics, back to God, and finally to his own legacy.

Two things have happened as a result of America electing its first African American president. It has shown how far we've come as a nation. And it shows how far we still have to go.

Grady paused there, took a white handkerchief from his coat pocket and wiped his head. He looked up and around at the audience, put his handkerchief away, and after a few moments, continued.

Never before in history of the office of the president has the president been so disrespected. Racism is still alive and well. Each one of us must be willing to confront it whenever and wherever it raises its ugly head. You see it takes the black keys and white keys to play the Star-Spangled Banner.

In order for us to continue moving forward with dignity and respect, we must get back to God...When I reach the end of my journey, no one will gather at a civic center to celebrate my birthday, but I pray that someone, somewhere would gather around a dinner table and thank God for the difference made in their lives because I passed that way.

* * *

After Grady completed his speech and the night's celebration for Dr. King had ended, many people who heard him stayed to talk to him and Kathleen. They were old friends, colleagues, and even judges who remembered him years earlier in court when he was living another kind of life. For the past four years Grady has been the pastor at New Mercy Baptist Church in Griffin, Georgia, and leading the kind of life, doing God's work in helping others, for which he hopes to be remembered. He's making a difference in the lives' of others. His journey continues.

ELEVEN

Daphne Caldwell Rackley was the first of three children born to Grady and Kathleen Caldwell, and when she was young, it became confusing to her when things began disappearing from her family home. The confusion led to pain and anger. There was the pool table, her mother's pearl necklace, and then the television set in Daphne's bedroom. They would all go. All very odd she thought then as a young girl.

Born in 1969, Daphne was a "daddy's girl," and in the beginning her father made her laugh, played tennis with her, and even taught her karate, having learned that martial art himself. It required tough mental discipline. He sought the same for his daughter. Daphne said she didn't remember her father changing diapers or doing yard work. He was the "fun parent" in her world while Kathleen later provided the discipline and structure, stressing the importance of school, good behavior, and faith in God. By the time family belongings were mysteriously leaving, Grady's own mental discipline, once sharp, had been replaced by drug addiction.

"I do remember things disappearing in our house. Like the pool table. Momma said it was broken, but later I found out Daddy pawned it to buy drugs," Daphne said.

It was June 17, 2012, Father's Day, when Daphne told me her story about growing up and her passage into adulthood. Before we began our interview at Grady and Kathleen's home outside of Griffin, Daphne was in the kitchen with her mother preparing ears of yellow corn to be cooked for the afternoon meal. Daphne was wearing a pink blouse and shorts and stood over the kitchen sink, laughing and smiling with her mother. They looked perfect together. Daphne's brother, Grady Caldwell III and sisters, Carmen and Yolanda, were there, too. Grandchildren were in the house for the Father's Day meal. Later Grady would open gifts. There was a lot of joy that day in the Caldwell home. Most of the time when Kathleen and Grady's children were young, back in Albany, it wasn't that way. Families change. Strong ones, with God's help, stay together. Daphne continued talking about her childhood.

"There was a period of time when we hid everything from Daddy. We would hide our purses, money, checkbooks. Everything," Daphne said. "I came home once and my TV was gone. My Grandmother Leola went to the pawn shop and got it out."

Leola Caldwell spent years covering for the misdeeds and decadence of her son. Getting Daphne another television surprised no one who knew her. For Daphne there would be other surprises beyond the disappearance of family belongings. It wasn't until "the tenth or eleventh grade" when she began to understand the depths of her father's addiction and reckless behavior. Once, she visited him in the hospital after he was beaten in a fight. He looked awful. She was worried about him dying. Until her high school years, she said she believed her father's absences, sometimes for weeks at a time, were work related. Kathleen, the always protective mother, told her children this. It wasn't true. Their father spent periods away from the family while high on drugs and having sex with other women. That was the truth. Kathleen knew but didn't want her children to know. In that same bedroom where Grady had taken Daphne's television and pawned it to buy drugs, she would sometimes cry late at night and ask God to help her daddy. She wanted her daddy back to the way he once was.

When Daphne was in grade school her father had her separating the marijuana seeds from the leaves before he put the leaves in rolling paper, lit it and got high in front of her. He told her it was tobacco. What's a ten-year-old going to do? Believe her father. And she did until one day at school where she was a sixth grader at Lincoln Heights, law enforcement officers conducted a drug awareness program for the students. Daphne was well behaved and attentive. Just what her parents had taught her to do. The Caldwell children were expected to do well and contribute to "society in big ways," Daphne said. During the program she became worried and scared for her father now knowing what he was smoking, with her help, was not tobacco. When the program ended she was walking toward one of the officers to inform him about her father's marijuana smoking, but before she could reach him, she was called to her bus that would take her home. She worried the rest of the day. After school she told her mother that her father was smoking dope and he could hurt himself and even go to jail. That's what the law officers said, Daphne told her mother.

"Momma convinced me not to worry. She said everything was going to be all right, that Daddy was all right. Momma had a way of making me feel better," Daphne said. "And she always covered up for him. She never degraded him. Other people may have, but she never did."

Kathleen could make things, and did for a long time, seem better than they actually were. She worked hard to protect her children and disguise the truth. For many years that's what she did. The truth, in the end, will have the final say. Painful or joyous, it always has the final say. God will ensure that.

"I grew up thinking we were like the Bill Cosby family (television's ideal African American family of the 1980s). Momma and Daddy did a good job of never arguing in front of us," Daphne said. "It was a stable home life. I never knew there were serious issues until I was in high school."

As she continued her story, I could hear loud talk and laughter and children playing in another part of the house. The Father's Day meal would soon be served, and there were gifts for her father to open. It was a happy day, but her story wasn't. During the bad years, Daphne said her mother was a "workaholic," both to provide for the family as her husband spent thousands of dollars on drugs and to focus her thoughts away from the awful pain Grady was causing. "We never went without. Momma took care of us," Daphne said.

One of the first times Daphne recalled being hurt and even angry toward her father was after reading a letter her mother had written to Grady. He had been away from the family for weeks, living with his girlfriend in Hazlehurst and stoned on crack cocaine. In the letter, Kathleen admonishes Grady for buying a bicycle for his girlfriend's child. Kathleen was angry and so was Daphne to learn of this at a time when Grady was providing little or no financial support for his own family. He was living his life as a taker, not a giver.

"I still remember how upset I was toward him then. Momma was doing everything to keep our family together and then I learned about the bike. It hurt me," Daphne said.

Daphne's understandable anger stayed with her for years, only to deepen as her father was in and out of drug rehabilitation clinics and in and out of jail and prison for the crimes committed to buy the drugs. She had little contact with him during this period. She didn't want to see him in such a way. Daphne was hurt, embarrassed, and disappointed in her father, a man with so much promise. She did not exchange letters with him. He tried at times, but she refused to write. She went about two years without any contact with him at all during his drug years. Could she ever forgive him for what he did to his family? For the suffering he caused her mother? Daphne visited him only once when he was in these other places and not home where he should've been. She saw him when he was an inmate at the Jefferson Correctional Institute in Louisville, Georgia, by the late 1990s.

The three-hour drive northeast from Albany was significant in another way. It was the first time she had time with her "newly-discovered" sister, Yolanda. The entire drive was spent "getting to know one another," she said. "I remember thinking that it's amazing how there are really things like family secrets. Discovering that she knew my grandmother as *her* grandmother without us ever knowing of or encountering one another was and in some ways still is unimaginable." Daphne's trip to see her father in prison became more than that in the end.

"Before the trip, I used to feel almost sick when I would think of the way Yolanda must have felt, especially when she knew about us but we didn't know about her," Daphne said. "After the trip I could feel the magnificent sovereignty of God. In that car I didn't hear bitterness, which would've been understandable. I heard an openness and willingness to be vulnerable. What a miracle. This was definitely a trip to see my father and my Father."

Daphne and Yolanda visited their father in the same place I had met Grady when I interviewed him for my book, *Made or Broken: Football & Survival in the Georgia Woods*. Louisville was the last place he was incarcerated. When they left that day, Daphne said she had little hope he would ever change. She was even surprised, after all the dangerous things he had put himself through, that he was still alive. Maybe God was watching over him. He had long since been the "fun parent."

Daphne encouraged her mother, and sometimes pleaded with her, to divorce her father and create a new and better life for herself. He was the one causing all the pain, all the tears. Kathleen refused and kept faith in God that she was doing the right thing by not divorcing Grady. Kathleen Jones Caldwell was a strong and beautiful woman who should leave Grady and find someone she could create a loving and caring relationship with, Daphne said. Certainly God would understand if Kathleen did file for divorce.

"I knew she was hurt, but she didn't have peace with divorce. Momma showed us what faith in God means. What *real* faith means," Daphne said. While Kathleen's strength was a lesson in love and faith in God, the many years of Grady's drug addiction showed the workings of a "self-absorbed" parent. His drugs were more important than family love. He was a trickster, too. Grady went to rehab several times, and each time he got out he said he was better, but his eyes spoke differently, Daphne said.

"He was good at fooling people, but when he got out of Hampton,

I saw a different Daddy," Daphne said. "I remember saying, 'This is it, Momma. This is it.' "

Grady's last stay in a rehabilitation setting was in Hampton, Georgia, just south of Atlanta, in the early 2000s. Since then he has not used drugs. Since then he has worked to restore his life and family. For Daphne, there have been times when her life was in need of restoration, of God's help. It had been longstanding, too. "I went through my own spiritual crisis. I'm not sure it was related to Daddy's problems or not, but I had my own struggles," Daphne said.

By the late 1980s she had graduated from Monroe High School in Albany, Georgia, was an excellent student, and was expected by her family to go to college as her parents had done. The anger toward her father and his drug-induced behavior kept building during her high school years and into college. She was accepted into Georgia Tech in Atlanta, studied little and dropped out during a time she called her "rebellious years."

After dropping out of Georgia Tech, Daphne eventually enrolled at Southern Polytechnic State University in Marietta, Georgia, and there she found the academic discipline that she lost at Tech. Her rebellious days were over, she said. Daphne studied hard and looked to the future, trying not to become engulfed in what her father was doing to himself and his family. It was difficult sometimes to stay focused, but she did. She graduated with a degree in mechanical engineering by the early 1990s. Daphne fell in love and married Ernesto Rackley, they have one child together, Asia Simone Rackley, and today live in Fairburn, Georgia, just south of Atlanta. In 2006 she began working with the City of Atlanta's Department of Watershed Management, and in 2010 she became deputy chief information officer for the city's Department of Information Technology.

"I think the biggest thing from what Daddy put us through is you can't change anyone. We kept trying to rescue him. Everybody tried to save him. They (addicts) have to learn the lesson themselves. But on the other side is to have faith that redemption can occur. I've seen it," Daphne said.

Has she fully forgiven her father? Is that even possible? "I don't have that anger anymore. I just have questions. For our family to be where we are now – I wouldn't have seen it. I didn't expect it," Daphne said.

From the other rooms I still heard laughter, loud talking, and three young grandchildren of Grady and Kathleen's running through the house playing hide-and-go-seek. I heard Grady's full voice in storytelling and laughter. It was ringing throughout the house.

* * *

Seven years after Daphne was born, Grady and Kathleen had another girl, Carmen, who many years removed from her childhood today still struggles emotionally with the kind of father and husband Grady was during those dark years, drug years. She continues down the road to full reconciliation with her father. Life is much better, but there are still periods of difficulty. "I'm going through counseling now. We have been going back to that time of my life so everything is fresh and at the forefront of my mind. The reason I'm stuck, my counselor says, it's related to *that,*" Carmen said.

"THAT" would be what she experienced growing up in the Caldwell home, a place where she remembers when she was five or six, her dad tickling her belly until she laughed and laughed and could hardly breathe. The laughter didn't last long.

"I don't have a lot of great memories," Carmen said.

Some of her memories are full of fear, others evoke hurt, and there is a lot of suffering. She was, nearly all the time, embarrassed by her father's behavior.

"I remember one time a drug dealer came to our house. I was about 10 or 11, and my dad was trying to tell him to leave" when his children were around. She was afraid that day, and there were other times like that, too. Her little-girl-life had been stolen from her.

"I remember him being home but not present. I remember feeling that we (her sister and brother) were in the way," Carmen said. "Saturday mornings we'd want to watch cartoons, but he'd come in and watch westerns. It was all about him."

Like Daphne, Carmen attended Monroe High School in Albany where one of her friends was a drug dealer who had been approached by Grady seeking to buy dope. Carmen's friend knew it was her father. He refused to sell to him, but he told Carmen all about it. "I remember when that happened being so embarrassed. I said, 'You should've sold it to him and made that money.' I was torn. I was so angry," she said.

Once she was working at JC Penney in the Albany Mall and saw her father come in her department. He pulled a shirt off a display rack and intending to falsely return the shirt, get cash from the store and buy drugs. This was typical for Grady during this time. Grady saw his daughter and went to her cash register. She explained the situation to a co-worker, needing authorization before accepting a return item. She took the shirt and gave cash to her father, both stealing from the store and enabling his drug use. She was emotionally upset because of seeing her father and what she had done. She felt bad.

"I did it and gave him the money just to get him to leave. I cried about it in the store. I could've lost my job," Carmen said.

There would be a lot more crying for years to come.

When she made money at JC Penney and other part-time jobs, Carmen would often hide it under her mattress in her bedroom in efforts to keep her father from coming into her room at night, stealing her money, and buying drugs with it. A peaceful sleep she rarely had.

One day when she was home, she was a teenager then, she heard a rare argument, very loud, between her mother and father. The commotion was coming from their bedroom. It was getting louder and louder. She was always concerned about her mother and went into the room to help. She knew the drugs had been doing bad things to her father. Carmen ran into their bedroom with her hairbrush in her hand and began using it to hit her father. Finally, after being hit several times by Carmen, Grady released the hold he had on his wife

"Momma was screaming, 'You won't take the keys!' And Daddy was trying to pull the car keys out of her hands. They were on the floor," Carmen said. "She was holding so tight to the keys her hands were bleeding. He wanted to take our car to get drugs. Momma didn't want him to go."

Kathleen finally threw the car keys at Grady who picked them up from the floor and "left out with me running behind him screaming at him," Carmen said.

When Carmen learned about her father's long-term girlfriend in Hazlehurst, she told her mother to divorce her father so he wouldn't "take her for granted anymore." Then if Grady did quit using drugs, became a responsible adult again, the two could consider re-marrying. That was Carmen's plan, and she pushed hard for it, always concerned about her mother's well-being. Carmen had had enough, but Kathleen refused to consider seriously a divorce. It was the same response she had given Daphne who urged her mother to do the same.

Of the three Caldwell children, Carmen said she was "the most rebellious" toward her father for years as he seemed intent on destroying his life and causing those who loved him to suffer. From rehab clinics, jail, and prison, Grady wrote Carmen trying to keep the communication open with his youngest daughter, always asking for forgiveness, and always claiming he'd do better next time. She said she wrote him only one letter during all the years he was away from his family. "I was just very flippant with him. It was all so hurtful," Carmen said. There's still some pain in her eyes from the hurt of years ago.

Changes finally began to occur within Grady while Carmen was living in Seattle in the early 2000s. Carmen, as did her older sister Daphne, made good grades in school, as expected. She graduated from Albany State University in 1998 with a biology degree and was hired by the Environmental Protection Agency in Seattle. There she earned a master's degree in public administration at the University of Washington. However, something began to happen within her. God was calling her in another direction, and she accepted the call. While working for the EPA, she began working in the ministry in Seattle. Carmen also began to receive news from her family in Georgia about her father's recovery, and "changes were happening and I wasn't witnessing it," she said.

Carmen returned in 2007 and began working with Grady and Kathleen at his church, New Mercy Baptist Church in Griffin, and she moved in and is still living with her parents in their redbrick home in the Wellington subdivision on US Highway 19, just outside of the city. Today she's youth pastor for the church. In December 2010 she earned a master's degree in divinity from the McAfee School of Theology at Mercer University in Atlanta. It's a new way of living as a family with a sober father, one with his own church to pastor. Still there's the past. It's always close by.

Working with her father daily Carmen's still sees signs of "self-absorbed behavior," but not the kind that almost killed him and wounded deeply her family.

"I have forgiven him but had to do my own processing. The anger doesn't control me anymore. I had a lot of anger issues once," Carmen said. What she does know is she's devoting her life to God's work while continuing to seek counseling for her own spiritual well-being. The road of spiritual nourishment is not without strife. The road can be long.

"I think God has done a great work in the restoration of our family," Carmen said. About her father, "he has accepted fully his actions, but I don't think he understands the impact of it all. I don't think he fully gets it." Understanding leads to empathy and for that, in some ways, Carmen awaits.

* * *

This will not be a surprise. The third and last child of Grady and Kathleen, Grady Lee Caldwell III born in 1980, has only a few good memories as a young boy being around his father and by the time he was out of middle school, he had developed a deep resentment toward him - the same kind of feeling that troubled his two sisters. Before things turned bad, Grady did teach his only son karate and encouraged him to follow his passion in sports. It was a good father-son-relationship in the beginning. Grady knew about sports and knew how tough you had to be to play well. Grady risked his own personal safety to be on the Albany High team in the 1960s. He had been a good swimmer, too. The two had, like many fathers and sons, found a bond through athletic competition. Lee figured early on that whatever games he chose to play, his father would be there watching him. It would not be that way.

Grady told his son little of what he had helped accomplish in the 1960s and '70s through sports and political activism. Nor did he talk much about civil rights history, knowing and being around Dr. Martin Luther King, Jr., when he came to Albany. Grady had lived through and contributed to one of the most turbulent racial periods in American history. He had a powerful story to tell, but Lee wouldn't learn much about it through his father.

"People in the community talked about my daddy. They'd say, 'Your daddy was one of the smartest black guys I know,' but he never really shared that much with me. He never talked much about the good things he had done in the past," Lee said.

When Lee became old enough to ask questions about his father's absence from the family, his mother tried to cover by saying his father had a lot of work to do out of town. This satisfied Lee for a short period. Then things began to occur in their home that Lee saw and wished he had not. His father was regularly using crack cocaine at their house, locking himself in his bathroom to do so. By then Lee could not be fooled by his mother's attempts at deception.

"I can remember him getting stoned at home. He'd come out of the bathroom sweating like crazy, and I remember a mark on the sink from the crack pipe. I still remember the smell of the air. To this day I remember how it smelled," Lee said. He described it as putrid, sickening.

During these years Kathleen would often call him from work, concerned about her children and husband. "Momma would say, 'Is your daddy there? Is everybody all right? Is your daddy all right'?" Lee said. When his father was home, many times he wasn't all right, and young Lee knew that.

With growing resentment and hurt because of his father's behavior, the two became involved in what Lee called a "physical altercation" when he was about 12 or 13. Lee's memory is not clear today on what he did or said to provoke his father, who "slammed me down pretty good." Grady didn't hit his son. Kathleen was at home when it happened and saw the two wrestle but did not attempt to stop the argument between her husband and son. Lee, now a father himself, said as troubled and irresponsible as his father was back then, "he was still my father," and a son's respect toward his father still mattered. But by then Lee's respect for his father could've been measured in a thimble, if recognized at all. Any signs of self-respect Grady had had disappeared.

"My resentment started out as embarrassment. A guy I knew told me once, 'Yeah, I saw your daddy in jail.' I was used to seeing my daddy on top, not in jail," Lee said.

During his father's time of rehab, jail, and prison, several years, Lee had little communication with him. Each time his dad was incarcerated or did something foolish because of his drug addiction, the embarrassment and resentment boiled inside of the only son. There was something else that worsened the hurt back then. "I got the same name he's got. You know what I mean?" Lee said. He told me his story the same day as did his sisters, Daphne and Carmen. The pattern of their lives became easy to discern. Pain and love crisscrossed the living and telling of it all.

"I reached a point years ago where I realized that drugs mess up some of the best people. You can call it what you want, but the devil's going to go after the best," Lee said.

His five-year-old son Grayson came into the room where we were talking as he was looking for a place to hide from his cousin. They were playing hide-and-go-seek. Lee, in a soft voice, suggested another room in the house. "Okay, Daddy. I'll go there," Grayson said.

All three of Kathleen and Grady Caldwell's children, in telling their stories, come back to their mother. It's her they worried the most about. All three stories evoke a woman with a beautiful heart. "I was very protective of my mother, but didn't ever suggest, like Daphne and Carmen, that she divorce our father," Lee said. He worried about her, prayed for her, asking God to give her strength through her ordeal with his father. At night lying in bed he'd think about his mother and the emotional strain his father was causing her. Any child that loves his mother would do the same. It would all end one day, he thought. It just had to.

"She was a first-class mother. She handled it about as well as anybody could. For a long time she was just trying not to give up on him...Momma made sure I had my priorities right," Lee said. Kathleen used fear occasionally to instill the correct priorities as Lee was coming of age with a father of little help in modeling the right path into manhood. It was up to her to discipline the children. What could Grady do? She had a husband who couldn't discipline himself.

One day at Highland Middle School in Albany, Lee was in the sixth or seventh grade, and his unruly behavior caused the administrators to telephone Kathleen. Caldwell children were supposed to know the value, the importance of being well behaved and working hard in school. They had a family tradition that reflected such manners. That day young Lee had apparently forgotten what he had been taught. After receiving the phone call, Kathleen left her job at Albany State, drove to Highland, picked Lee up and drove home and took him inside.

"She told me to take my clothes off. I told her I wasn't going to. She said, 'I'm going to call the police.' She picked up the phone and before she got to the last number, I had my clothes off. She used the belt on me again. My dad was in jail then. I didn't want to go to jail," Lee said.

She drove Lee back to school where his behavior was exemplary the rest of the day and for many days to come. He worked hard in middle school and never again was a troublemaker in class, he said. Threat of jail worked. That's where his dad was and he wasn't going to end up there. He was certain about that.

He attended Westover High School in Albany, and during his freshman year, his dad took him to a tattoo parlor where he got a tattoo of the Toronto Raptor mascot of the National Basketball Association on his arm. "Momma didn't want me to get it," Lee said. Throughout his high school years, when he did well academically and athletically, his father would not be there. Lee kept his passion for sports that he learned from his dad and developed into one of the top athletes in South Georgia, receiving scholarship offers in both football and basketball. His father attended very few of his games. When Lee led Westover to a basketball state championship his senior year, his dad did not see the game.

Grady said he couldn't remember if he was "in prison, jail or getting high" when the game was played.

Kathleen said, to the best of her memory, he was not in prison or jail but using drugs at the time and "probably looked so bad he was too embarrassed to come to the game."

Lee accepted a basketball scholarship at Albany State University and earned a degree in health and physical education from there. He played ball all four years, but his father saw only two games. The games his father attended were during Lee's senior season in 2001. That passion was in full bloom on the court both times. Lee scored 38 points against Clayton State University and 28 against Morehouse College. His father had been released from the Jefferson County Correctional Institute, the last time he was incarcerated. Back then Grady was beginning the long walk to recovery. He had miles to go for there was much pain in the roads behind him.

Through his high school and college years, if someone Lee knew asked about his dad and drugs, he had a repetitive reply: "He's a dealer not a crack head," Lee said. He told me that among some of his African American friends, being a drug dealer is "better than being a crack head." Not something you're proud of, either way, but one may be a bit better than the other.

Today Lee is married, has one child and is an assistant principal at Mary Pearson High School in Forsyth, Georgia. While in education he has earned a graduate degree at Georgia College and State University at Milledgeville. He and his family live in Byron, not far from Griffin, making it easy for him to regularly visit his parents, as he did on that Father's Day. He agreed with his sister Daphne that redemption can and has occurred within their family. The process is ongoing.

"I have stopped holding a grudge against him. Yeah, I wish he could've been there more during my playing days...I think my dad got caught up in the social aspect of drugs and it took him a long time to get out," Lee said.

For the son, as awful as the father was for many years, he sees himself in the father. "I was a popular guy like my dad was. He was a leader and I am too," Lee said. Sons see themselves in the father often hoping to find what's best. Grady Lee Caldwell III was no different from other sons.

TWELVE

Ronda Swartz was wearing a long blue shirt and jeans as she smoked a cigarette across the street from New Mercy Baptist Church after praying and talking with Grady inside. Something terrible had recently happened in her life. She had come to Pastor Grady, like many others, seeking his guidance. It was a late summer afternoon in 2012, and the sky was blue like her shirt and almost cloudless as a breeze blew cool that day. Ronda lives in the church's neighborhood and said about two weeks earlier her best friend had been stabbed to death. That's why she had come to see Grady. She needed his help.

A few minutes before I spoke with Ronda outside the church, I overheard her speaking with Grady in the church sanctuary. Bible study was scheduled for the evening, and members were coming in, talking to one another, and beginning to take their seats where they hear Grady preach on Sundays. I could see Ronda was upset and crying. Grady reached for and held both her hands as they stood near one of the doors in the sanctuary, away from those coming in and sitting down. I could hear most of what they said. "These are my problems, these are my stumbling blocks," Ronda said.

Grady began asking God to come into her heart and give her comfort in this time of grief and loss. He told God she had come to Him today because in her own life "she has come to a point of brokenness" and is asking God to restore her, make her whole again. Grady's prayer with her lasted a couple of minutes, and the whole time he had both of her hands in his. When he finished asking for God's intercession, he told Ronda he loved her and for her to call anytime and come back to the church to see him whenever she needed. He would be there for her. Ronda thanked him, hugged him and slowly walked out of the church to light her cigarette. After she left, Grady said to me: "We deal with hurting folks."

Ronda, now outside and eyes red from crying, had known hurt for some years. She was white, 42 years old, and had been recently paroled out of prison after spending four years there for burglary, she said. She and Grady often talk about what it was like in prison, how to survive and look to the future for a better life, all with the hand of God. Now her best friend had been killed. She had been coming to New Mercy for about a year, not always for Sunday school or church service, but always to see Grady, talk with and sometimes pray with him. Coming to New Mercy always makes her feel better, she said. She pulled hard on her cigarette and pushed her salt-and-pepper hair off her forehead. She wiped tears from her eyes.

"When I feel like I can't see no other way, something makes me come to New Mercy. Everything works out. I always feel better when I leave…Having a preacher that's been down the same road I have been down helps me…I've never completely surrendered myself to God. Pastor Grady taught me how to surrender and still teaches me. He taught me that things done in the past are in the *past*," Ronda said. She took another pull from her cigarette, rubbed her eyes again and looked toward the church where more people were arriving for Bible study.

* * *

New Mercy Baptist Church is at 742 Pimento Avenue in Griffin, and it evolved out of a home-Bible study group in 2007 of about a dozen believers led by Grady. He had left his position in the ministry at Zion Baptist in Hampton, just north of Griffin, and was following the Lord's calling. He had no church and his Bible study group was growing. The city of Griffin owned the 6,500 square-foot building that became New Mercy and over the years it had been used as a police community center, an elementary school, and it once served as a site for Head Start, the federally-funded program that helps impoverished children. Grady approached city officials about the building, and they agreed to a five-year lease for a dollar a year. By 2008 Grady now had a building, one that needed a lot of work, but he had a building. He conducted his first service at New Mercy June 8, 2008. From about a dozen at his original Bible study group, by the summer of 2012 New Mercy had about 170 active members. In December 2011 the church took full ownership of the building paying the city $50,000 for it.

On some Sundays, with a growing congregation, there is not enough room to accommodate everyone in the sanctuary. Grady and church leaders have leased from a businessman a redbrick building across the street from New Mercy, for 20 years and a dollar a year. That building is about 7,000 square foot. Eventually it will be used as the sanctuary. Plans call for the current building, once the larger building is renovated, to house community service and youth activities. New members continue to come.

Old, rusted barbed wire fences surround vacated buildings near New Mercy, and across Pimento Avenue is a boarded up redbrick building with a large sign that says, Green Front Café, Enjoy Coca-Cola. About a quarter mile from the church, Pimento intersects with Meriwether Street where there's a large public housing complex bordered by a tall, black iron fence. This is a very poor neighborhood.

Griffin's 2010 population was about 24,000 of which about half are African Americans. Grady's church is predominately African American but it does include about "seven to 10 percent" white members, like Ronda Swartz, he said. About a fifth of the city's residents live below the poverty line set by the federal government. Grady and his church leaders see the suffering related to poverty. It is all around them. The 2010 median family income was $33,863. Griffin is about an hour's drive south of Atlanta, and US Highway 19 cuts through it, north and south. During the Civil War the Confederate government printed money in Griffin, but it was worthless after the surrender of the South in 1865. Railroad lines during the war brought in trainloads of sick and wounded Confederate soldiers. For decades after the war it was a textile mill town, but as in much of the South, those jobs have gone. The biggest private employer today is Caterpillar Inc., with around 900 workers. It's poverty that defines the neighborhood where Grady, his wife Kathleen, and daughter Carmen have decided to do God's work.

* * *

Paul and Ann Sutton married in 1990 and met Grady at Zion Baptist Church in Hampton where he served as assistant pastor and where Paul had been a member for 38 years and a deacon. He's retired from Ford Motor Company, and Ann works for CVS Pharmacy in

Jonesboro. They were eager to tell me their story. Both said they'd never had a minister like Grady. "When I first met him, he was outstanding. He was a very caring and concerned person. He cared about people. He was just a beautiful person who was led by the Spirit," Ann said.

Paul and Ann were two of the original members of New Mercy and still live in Hampton, about a 25-minute drive from their new church. He's a deacon at New Mercy and she's an evangelist. God called them to a new home, they both said. They come to New Mercy two or three times a week and sometimes on Saturday mornings when along with Grady and other members they walk through the housing projects sharing the Word of God. There are suffering people who need to hear the Word and feel love from Grady and New Mercy, Paul and Ann said. It is their calling.

"We show love and embrace people where they are. It doesn't matter if its alcohol or drugs, no matter where you been or how you smell. It's about love. That's from Pastor Grady...It's all about love and caring for folks," Ann said.

Ann and Paul were sitting next to one another in one of the classrooms at New Mercy where the love of Jesus and the New Testament is taught. It reflects the same kind of powerful, nourishing, and overwhelming love that Kathleen showed Grady and her family during all those years when drugs and selfish behavior consumed her husband. That kind of love now emanates from New Mercy. Kathleen is volunteering there as church administrator, Carmen is there, and Grady is there. He told me more than once during our many interviews together that "learned how to love through Kathleen." To know Grady's story and to know Kathleen is to know that *is* the truth. I've been around few people in my life like Kathleen Jones Caldwell. The first time I met her more than 12 or 13 years ago when Grady was still in prison, I realized then her deep sense of love and humanity. It can be a model for others. Since then, after spending several hours with her and talking with those who know her well, I've only reaffirmed my initial impression. The Caldwell family spent years in heartache, and it manifests itself in one way today in a deep, rich love for others. That *should* be the calling of the church: Love and only love. Where Jesus is, love is. Grady often reminds me of that.

With Grady's story, his personal testimony, and his emphasis on a loving ministry, Paul said he expects the church will continue to grow. The challenges to help others are many. "There is a lot of hardship and poverty in this community," Paul said.

Grady's willingness to share, in full honesty, his life story, the devotion of Kathleen, who Paul called "a beautiful person full of love, and Carmen's work with the youth" have created something Paul had not witnessed before. "You talk about a testimony. These two people (Grady and Kathleen) love people and love God...It's a powerful ministry. I've been in church all my life and never seen anything like it," Paul said.

* * *

There was a time in Arthur Atkins' life when he drank a lot of alcohol, spent time "on the streets" doing things he later regretted, and neglecting important things, the things the Lord wanted from him. He was not following God's path. He admitted all that to me in telling a story not unlike Grady's. Arthur works for the Spalding County Parks and Recreation Department, lives outside of Griffin, and he and his wife Susie have two sons. Like Paul and Ann, Arthur first heard Grady preach at Zion Baptist. And like the Suttons, Arthur was both impressed and inspired by Grady and followed him to New Mercy where he is a deacon today. Grady's story was what attracted Arthur. It was a common theme among those I interviewed at New Mercy.

"He told us about his drugs and he had been in prison. He was honest about it. I could relate to that because I've been through some things, too," Arthur said... "Honesty is what I liked about him. He was just honest about the mistakes he made."

Arthur was born in 1952 and remembered what his father told him about preachers: Beware of the ones who holler when they are preaching. Sometimes loud and overbearing preachers speak that way to hide their own lack of sincerity and authenticity. Not Pastor Grady, Arthur said, "he doesn't holler and he's not a prosperity preacher."

Arthur explained that a prosperity preacher is one who is more concerned about asking God to provide wealth and economic security instead simply using the love of God to love and help your fellow man. Arthur experiences the latter from Grady and New Mercy, and he sees a church that will continue to grow because of how Grady uses the Word to love and help others.

"I see us probably going to get way bigger. God's going to increase his harvest. That's why we're expanding across the street. We fill up on Sundays...Pastor Grady is a good preacher and teacher. He always has a smile and handshake," Arthur said.

* * *

Grady and New Mercy have received enormous help from the Georgia Baptist Convention and member churches in renovation efforts that led to the opening of his church. Those churches include Cornerstone Baptist Church in Lithia Springs, Zion Baptist Church of Hampton, New Salem Baptist, First Baptist, Second Baptist, Union

Baptist and Carver Road Baptist all of Griffin and Mt. Zion Baptist Church in Albany, Grady's childhood church.

Pastor Daniel Simmons of Mt. Zion said his church has given New Mercy about $3,000 annually since the church opened in 2008. He occasionally preaches at New Mercy, and Grady will do the same at Mt. Zion in Albany. In 2006, Grady spoke at Mt. Zion during the Church & Pastor Anniversary, which is "a big celebration for us. I wanted people to know that Grady was back (life restored) and that I endorse him and New Mercy." Pastor Simmons said Grady has established a spiritual "niche" being able to reach those suffering from drug and alcohol problems, both African American and white. "They don't see Grady in terms of race," he said. "They see him as a fellow traveler."

Pastor Simmons has known Grady and Kathleen since the 1970s and considers them close friends.

"In my mind Grady's reversal is nothing less than a miracle. His family relationships were restored," Pastor Simmons said. "His children love him. I think he and Kathleen are really a model couple of people being able to struggle well. Some of us don't struggle well. What Kathleen went through would've wiped most women out."

* * *

Volunteers from the partner churches installed a new roof, provided electrical work, updated New Mercy's air conditioning system, and provided other renovations to the building. Similar work is being done by these partner volunteers on the new building that was leased across the street. Grady views all of this as another sign of God's hand in what has been happening on Pimento Avenue. "The church wouldn't be possible without the Georgia Baptist Convention Basic Training provided by

Church Planting Ministries. Basic Training helped provide the tools to clarify the mission and vision, to put legs on the vision and develop partnerships to accomplish God's work," Grady said.

Teamwork at Pimento Avenue reminded Grady of what he learned on the football field in the 1960s at Albany High. Now instead of winning games, his efforts with the people around him are aimed at a higher calling. It's a calling from the Light of the Word. "Partnerships are vital. No one of us can do it alone. We need each other. Our mission is to go out in the power of Christ and seek the lost, disciple the found, and teach how to apply God's Word to everyday life," Grady said.

Ministries at New Mercy include an afterschool program for pre-k and six year olds, a computer lab, literacy training, a summer youth program, food pantry which serves about 90 families a month, a clothes closet providing for more than a 100 families each month, and an off-campus site for GED training. The needs are many in New Mercy's neighborhood.

Grady's daughter Carmen is the youth pastor and executive director of New Mercy Community Services and has led children from her church on field trips including to the Dr. Martin Luther King, Jr., Center in Atlanta and the Tellus Science Museum in Cartersville. Another field trip for Carmen and the children is through their own neighborhood. She leads them on walks observing the habits, both good and bad, of people and how to address their problems, how to make their lives better. She discusses ways with the children about how to develop good personal habits: honesty, a good work ethic, having discipline in school, a love for God, and to care for and love others.

"Our impact is to touch lives today for a better tomorrow. We do it for the families. We do it for children. We do it for the community," Carmen said. In January 2012 she spoke these words at the Kiwanis Club of Griffin while describing the many outreach programs at New Mercy. Her picture and the story about the church appeared on the front page of *The Griffin Daily News.*

As Carmen, Grady, Kathleen, and other church members are reaching out to the hurting and dispossessed, state Baptist leaders have been there to help New Mercy help others.

"So many from the Georgia Baptist Convention have helped us at New Mercy: Keith Hamilton in Church Financial Services, Stuart Lang with Baptist Builders, Steve Parr in Evangelism, Ricky Thrasher in Association Missions, and the entire Church Planting Team, Butch Butcher, Gerald Colbert, Galen Jones and Ben Lang," Grady said. All partners, all working through God.

Rev. Butch Butcher for five years has worked with the Georgia Baptist Convention Church Planting Team and said, "We need what's happening at New Mercy to happen all over the state. We are watching him closely. On some level he (Grady) is an emerging leader," one for the entire state. Butcher met Grady five years ago when he applied for membership into the Georgia Baptist Convention and shared in writing his testimony, including his criminal background. At the end of the lengthy process church leaders checked Grady's references and were "impressed" by what they learned and by his devotion to God and the Word.

Until recently the state's Southern Baptist leaders have not worked hard at ministering to African Americans, particularly those living near or in poverty, Butcher said. They are now focused on being more aggressive with new African American churches and outreach programs among neighborhoods like the one being served by Grady at New Mercy. There has been a change "for the better" among white Baptist leaders and how they see themselves in the context of God, the Word, and race, Butcher said. He has worked closely with Grady and New Mercy since the church opened in June 2008.

Butcher's job with the Georgia Baptist Convention is to help "plant English-speaking churches – African American and Anglo." Jerry Baker oversees the work of planting all non-English speaking churches for the state's Baptist Convention and over the past few years the two departments have planted about 55 churches annually, of which about 35 are English speaking, Butcher said.

"Grady has the unique ability to reach the down-and-outers," Butcher said. For Butcher the down-and-outers are the poor, the drug addicts, and the ones who feel life has whipped them below the ground and God has forsaken them. These are Grady's people. "He's a great preacher, teacher, and counselor. Number one he loves the Lord, and he's not trying to build a kingdom for himself" but is in the ministry for the service of others.

Many of the down-and-outers, those who are hurting and need the nourishment of the scripture, at New Mercy are African Americans but traditionally the Georgia Baptist Convention has been composed of predominately white middle-class members, Butcher said. Grady's work represents a new spiritual approach for state Baptist leaders that can be traced to 1995. That year the Georgia Baptist Convention formally and publicly apologized for its support of African American slavery. The issue of slavery in the 1800s first split the southern Baptist from their northern counterparts and then split a country. Today things are different and not just a little. In 2012 Rev. Fred Luter became the first African American to be chosen as president of the Southern Baptist Convention, which has about 16 million members of which about 20 percent are minorities. He is pastor of the Franklin Avenue Baptist Church in New Orleans.

African American members and leadership will continue to grow within the Southern Baptist Convention, Butcher said. This is a change many white members would've likely fought against just a couple of generations ago. Grady lived through those generations, and he's seen and contributed to some of the most compelling changes in civil rights history. Now he's part of another kind of change, one in which he hears clearly the call from God. "Grady is penetrating a group we have not had before" in terms of new members, Butcher said.

There are about 3,600 churches - only a small number are African American - that are members of the Georgia Baptist Convention today and they belong to 93 different associations. New Mercy is part of the Flint River Baptist Association, and it was churches of this association that helped renovate New Mercy before it opened. Today there are about 1.5 million Georgia members of the Southern Baptist Convention. During his years in church planting and since the time he entered the ministry about 25 years ago, Butcher, 56, has known many, many ministers throughout Georgia. Butcher said it's not just Grady's fall through drugs and rise with God's redemptive powers that marks him differently from many others in the ministry. Some of those ministers, just a few, have personal stories similar to Grady's of wayward living before the hand of God straightened a crooked path.

"Grady is rather exceptional," Butcher said. "Obviously he's an excellent preacher...You can be a great preacher and not have great character and integrity. He has great character and great integrity."

Butcher said the first time he and his wife Terri, they live in Monroe, Georgia, met Grady and Kathleen they "connected" and a friendship was quickly formed. They worked close together in preparing to open New Mercy. Butcher became impressed with Grady as he began by 2008 serving those who came to New Mercy and those living in the neighborhood.

"It was fascinating how God was using Grady to reach others who needed ministering," he said. Since the opening of New Mercy, Butcher often confers with Grady, asking his advice and suggestions in regards to other church plantings. Through God they developed both a good friendship and a good working relationship.

Grady is 63 years old, seven years older than Butcher, but he said he has "a lot in common with Grady," both having done other things before entering the ministry. For Grady there was business, politics, academia, and then drug addiction and prison. For Butcher, he worked in the construction business until he was 32 and then heard God's call into the ministry. He answered the call.

"I don't mean this as being critical, but a lot of pastors heard the call at 15" and have not done anything else with their lives besides the ministry, Butcher said. Sometimes, but not all the time, these pastors have a difficult time relating to other people. Men in particular, he said, sometimes respond better to pastors who have had other experiences outside the pulpit. Having worked in other fields, done other things with their lives – in Grady's case, illegal things – does help pastors better understand those they minister to, he said.

For Grady his testimony gives him keen insights in helping the "down-and-outers." God is calling the Georgia Baptist Convention in that direction, Butcher said.

* * *

Marcellus Blaylock was among those who left their church in Hampton, Georgia, and followed Grady to New Mercy. He saw in Grady the same qualities other members did like Arthur Atkins and Paul and Ann Sutton. Marcellus is a deacon at New Mercy and drives the church van picking up elderly, the young, and others who lack transportation and brings them to New Mercy for Bible Study and Sunday worship. He was born in 1943, still lives in Hampton, and he and his wife Christine have four children. He worked as a custodian for the Henry County Board of Education but is retired and spends a "good deal of time working at the church for the good of the community. They call it a tough community, but it's tough everywhere," Marcellus said.

There are plenty of challenges in doing God's work, he said. Drug addiction, poverty, illiteracy, and broken homes and broken hearts, can all be found right outside the church doors. "One of the community's big problems is that we have a lot of single parents out here. We need men in the homes," Marcellus said.

Grady was intent on opening a church in a neighborhood in such need of healing. "I give him an A-plus for that. He's a good teacher... He always talks about himself, his testimony, when he ministers in the neighborhood on weekends. He shares the Word that way and he reaches people," Marcellus said.

* * *

Hyson Driver was born in 1941 in Spalding County, Georgia, and was invited to Grady's Bible study group that had been organized before New Mercy Baptist Church opened. Hyson became interested in seeing and hearing Grady after a friend invited her to the study group. She would not be disappointed. She was surprised the first time she heard Grady and smiled broadly when she told me her story, smiled like a person who had found something good, something she had been for a long time looking.

"He's the type of man you can really put your trust in. When he teaches from the scripture, it overwhelms me," Hyson said. "That was the kind of man I was looking for in a minister. One that will tell you the truth. If he doesn't know, he'll tell you that too."

As I was talking to Hyson at New Mercy, Grady's daughter Carmen was greeting middle school children who had come to the church that evening for Bible study classes. I could hear some of them laughing and talking. Hyson had come to attend the adult classes. She was one of the first to join New Mercy and is in charge of its food pantry and clothes closet, open Saturdays from 10:00 a.m. to 1:00 p.m., and there to give help to the poor living in the neighborhood. This outreach program serves about 100 families a month.

Grady's compelling testimony of drug addiction and imprisonment are inspirational as he weaves the scripture into the telling, making "it stronger when he teaches us how to accept people. It helps you understand people." Remembering his own time of darkness, when he didn't follow the Word, allows him to better understand the troubled lives of some of the people the church serves, Hyson said.

"He tells us we can't look down on them. People that come in here for help and have been using drugs. He says, 'We have to show them love,'" Hyson said. It was the same kind of love she experienced from Grady when her life became troubled, uncertain. Not because of drugs. Doctors had diagnosed her with cancer.

Surgery was needed and several lymph nodes were removed and "two had cancer in them," she said. Today she is cancer free. She had chemotherapy and radiation treatments. She worried about her health, about dying. It was a time of reflection and prayer. Grady was there guiding her in prayer and comforting her.

"He gave me scripture to read each day, and we talked about it. He prayed with me and went to the doctor's appointments with me," Hyson said. "He visited me. Pastor Grady made me feel – just feel good. He helped me understand you go through *things* in life, but God's still there."

New Mercy is fortunate to have the Caldwell family, she said, "They have showed us all how to love."

I heard more voices and laughter from children coming into the church. Carmen was greeting them as they came in. Then Hyson Driver took me back to the first century after Christ had been crucified, a time of few believers. She compared Grady to one of that era's most determined Christian missionaries.

"He reminds me of Paul in the Bible because of his drive to teach people God's Word," Hyson said. "When Paul got converted he was driven to convert others. I think about Pastor Caldwell that way."

THIRTEEN

When Grady was in jail in the 1990s he wrote several letters to Kathleen, some I have included in this book, but one of the most revealing and even prophetic was dated November 9, 1995.

Dear Kat,

I feel a lot better since I first wrote you. God has chastened me good and really put the "fear of the Lord in me." I now understand what that means. He told me that He had to do it that way because I was treating the blood of Jesus as though it has no effect. I thought he was leaving me and turning me over to the tormentors, but He assured me that He still loves me and everything will be alright. He allowed me to get a glimpse of what it would be like without Him. He said that fear that I felt is the beginning of wisdom.

His mercy and grace is without measure. I've repented and turned away from my willful disobedience. He's renewed my joy and I look forward to each day and doing His will. Three were saved Sunday and the daily Bible study is growing. 8-12 each night.

...I don't know when I'll get out, but God has assured

me that everything will be alright. The way God is using me in here, Satan may try to kick me out of here any day now (smile)!

Tell my children I do love them and my life is not over yet. Thank God, He's not through with me yet and great and mighty things are forthcoming in Christ. Oh, I love you, too! You better not give up on me now, you'll miss your blessing (smile)!

Tell mom, thanks. I got the few dollars she sent. They really helped. I'm about to have more jail drawers than regular drawers and T-shirts (smile).

...Oh, if I get any mail from the Dept. of Labor or the Merck Company, open it and be prepared to fill me in. If it's for an interview, I'll try to push it back so I can make it.

This is my last stamp & envelope until I can get some more money in (smile) to buy some more.

Love,
Grady

Grady's "fear" of the Lord and his search for "wisdom" through that fear was something he often read about in the Bible during his time in jail.

He studied the book of Psalm Chapter 111 which states, "The fear of the Lord is the beginning of wisdom." In Proverbs Chapter Three: "Be not wise in thine own eyes; fear the Lord, and depart from evil."

When Grady writes to Kathleen about the "blood of Jesus," this evokes the suffering of Christ on the cross and the redemptive message of the Savior's crucifixion. Images and meaning through his Bible reading Grady knew, including from, 2 Corinthians Chapter One: 3-7:

Blessed be the God and Father of our Lord Jesus Christ, the Father of mercies and God of all comfort, who comforts us in all our tribulations that we may be able to comfort those who are in any trouble, with the comfort which we ourselves are comforted by God. For as the sufferings of Christ abounds in us, so our consolation also abounds through Christ. Now if we are afflicted, it is for your consolation and salvation, which is effective for enduring the same sufferings which we also suffer. Or if we are comforted, it is your consolation and salvation. And our hope for you is steadfast, because we know that as you are partakers of the sufferings, so also you will partake of the consolation.

In this letter Grady's journey through fear, suffering, and his hopefulness in acquiring wisdom is not the only theme. He speaks of deep family love, a longing to do right by the ones who love him the most, and to do God's work. All of that did come. At New Mercy Baptist Church in Griffin, Georgia, he has been able to transfer his strength through the years of suffering and fear, to love and compassion for those he serves. He may well have found the wisdom he had been seeking for all those years.

* * *

I had been in New Mercy Baptist a few times, but on July 8, 2012, I attended my first Sunday school class and worship service that began at 11 am. I wanted to see for myself what was attracting people to Grady and his new church. My wife Phyllis went with me. As a child her parents had taken her to Baptist churches and her memories of going there were not uplifting ones. Their messages were often ones based on "fear," she said. When she became an adult, she stopped attending. That day with me at New Mercy she found something different, something that *did* uplift her. The face of fear had disappeared.

"What I saw and heard – and felt – was all about love," Phyllis said. "I was welcomed by everyone. This was a totally different experience from what I had as a child."

* * *

Theo Harris was a tall African American with a gray goatee who wore a blue shirt and matching blue slacks. His shirttail was not tucked in his pants. He looked comfortable and at ease standing behind a podium in the sanctuary where seats were covered with burgundy cloth. There were about 15 to 20 adults attending the Sunday school class that had begun at 9:45 am. Theo had a Bible opened at the podium, and he quoted from Romans where "God's righteousness" is offered as a guide to believers and unbelievers alike. He spoke forcefully but not loud and overbearing. His language was clear, like a man used to speaking before others. "The most difficult thing to do is to accept Jesus Christ...Just surrender and open the door and let him in. And always do the right thing for the right reasons."

And always do the right thing. In years past, that had not been the life path of Grady.

After Theo's lesson and Sunday school ended, I introduced myself to him. I'm six feet tall and I looked straight up to him. He had a big smile and bigger handshake. Theo had been a member of New Mercy for about two years. He said he was an attorney and was originally from Massachusetts where he attended law school at Suffolk University in Boston. He practiced law for many years in Massachusetts including serving as a public defender in Boston. He was born in 1949 and had recently moved to the Griffin area where he has become executive director for a program backed by the Spalding County government called, "A Higher Calling." Its purpose is to find housing for men returning from prison. This was the same kind of help Grady needed about 12 years earlier. Theo said Grady is a member of the task force that helps his program and "right now we are housing 23" former prison inmates. The program seeks to "integrate these individuals back into the community" by helping them find jobs.

"What we need to do is change out anti-social group behavior for pro-social behavior," Theo said. "...I now practice preventive law."

After I had talked with Theo for a few minutes, people began entering the sanctuary for the 11 a.m. worship service. Some were dressed sharply in jackets and ties, nice dresses and pretty shoes. Others had on jeans and T-shirts, wore their shirttails out, and had dirty tennis shoes on their feet. Many carried Bibles into the sanctuary. Most were African American, but I saw a few whites among the congregation. There were young children holding the hands' of adults and some were being carried by adults. The sanctuary was small. Before the service ended, I counted about 100 worshippers.

Rev. Carmen Caldwell walked to the pulpit at that time and behind her were two large screens, both providing the church's vision and mission statement. "The vision of New Mercy Baptist Church is to be a body of believers in Jesus Christ that demonstrates the redemptive power of God's love by manifesting the principles of the Kingdom of God that will affect individuals, families, and the community." Appropriate, I thought, knowing Grady's life story. When songs were sung during the service, and there would be several, the words appeared on the screen. The music was both beautiful and reverberating. Rev. Carmen Caldwell, or "Rev. C.C." as she was referred to by some church members, spoke from the pulpit. "Let's prepare our minds to Jesus Christ and worship." She read from Psalm Chapter 92. "It's good to praise the Lord," she said. She then introduced Rev. Nadine Rountree, another ordained minister and the worship leader. Rev. Rountree had a microphone standing in front of the pulpit and began to lead in prayers and song. Her singing voice deep, rich, and remind me of the great singer, Aretha Franklin. Rev. Rountree was that good. It was one of the most beautiful voices I had ever heard in church or anywhere else.

People sang along with her, they sang with fullness enough to filter through the church doors, outside and to the sky above. The words of the song appeared on the screens. "Lord, prepare me to be a sanctuary, pure and holy, tried and true. With Thanksgiving, I'll be a living sanctuary for you." People were standing, singing, and clapping. Some swayed slightly to the right and back to the left with both hands extended over their heads. There was a lot of this, young and old alike. One woman not far from the pulpit had tears in her eyes. Before the service ended there would be others like her. By 11:10 a.m. the singing continued and people were still coming in. "Let the glory of God rise among us. Let the praise of our King rise among us." Those were the lyrics being sung, those were the words on the two big screens.

After about 15 minutes of Rev. Rountree leading in prayerful singing, love and emotion, I began to think that this is what it must've been like in African American churches all over the South during the Civil Rights Movement. This kind of emotional service was replicated many times during the 1960s, giving participants the strength they needed to march and confront danger. As I experienced the service at New Mercy, it reminded me, among other things, how important African American churches were in reshaping our country, and all for the better, too.

At about 11:15 a.m. Grady entered the church sanctuary from a door in front of the pulpit. As his guests that day, he sat next to me and Phyllis. Another song was being sung and words appeared on the screens. In a few moments the music stopped, and Rev. Carmen Caldwell returned to the pulpit.

"It feels good to be in God's house," she said. Then she introduced her father who came to the pulpit while his daughter sat behind him. Rev. Grady Caldwell began by introducing visitors, talking about an upcoming Bible school program for children, and making a few other church announcements. He wore a light brown suit meticulously pressed, light yellow shirt and tie and shoes shined well for the occasion. He wore glasses and a strap that secured them to his head. This was the first thing he said after the announcements: "If God can change me, everybody's got a chance." He smiled wide and looked down at his Bible after he said it. I saw heads nod up and down among the worshippers. They know his story. Maybe not the young children, but others do. Several times during our many interviews together Grady has said the exact same thing to me. *If God can change me, everybody's got a chance.* It's a teaching technique that he uses generously.

Now the sanctuary was quiet, the singing had ended, but there would be more before the service ended. One of the visitors Grady introduced was Travis Head, who was asked to come in front of the congregation and tell his story. Travis was a young man using a walker. He slowly came to the front of the church and began to speak. From July through December last year he had had two knee surgeries and two open-heart surgeries, Travis said. His medical bills had reached "one million dollars," he said. He became depressed, and a family member who is a member of New Mercy asked Grady to visit and pray with Travis, which he did. "I'm here today to tell you we're all going to have problems," Travis said. "The question is not whether God will answer our prayers but will we keep the faith."

Travis spoke for about five minutes about faith in God, never losing it, and how God calls His people to love everyone. That was the theme of the service. Rev. Grady Caldwell returned to the pulpit and thanked Travis for sharing his story. "I know that testimony spoke to someone here," Grady said. Then he asked the church deacons and ministers to come to the front of the pulpit. Next he asked anyone who was troubled, needed personal prayer and the comfort of the "Word," to come stand with the deacons. A few people got up from their seats and began walking to the deacons and ministers. For the next few minutes people in pairs, about a dozen total, were holding hands and praying together in front of the pulpit. Grady walked among those in prayer, touching them and blessing them. This became very emotional. I saw a couple of women crying. The praying continued. Heads were nodding up and down, some quick and rhythmically.

When this ended I saw an African American woman returning to her seat and using a handkerchief to wipe tears from her eyes. I saw a slender white woman wearing a pink blouse and pink and white pants carrying her Bible and returning to her seat. She was the last participant to leave the front of the church. Her body began to sway and one hand was swaying over her head; the other clutched the Bible. Then she stopped walking altogether and stood for a few moments. She began walking again with difficulty. Two men helped her to her seat. She had been overcome by the experience in front of the church, of praying and asking for God's help.

After the service ended, I spoke with the woman in the pink blouse, who said she had only been coming to New Mercy for a couple of weeks. She appeared to be in her 40s. She knew the neighborhood well. "This was my old user neighborhood," the place where she used to buy drugs. "I did a lot of things wrong back then," she said. "I did them many times over." Now she was coming back to the old neighborhood for a different reason. This time, she said, it was to find God's mercy.

When the worship resumed and those who had come in front of the pulpit returned to their seats, Rev. Rountree again led the gathering in another song. "Thank you Lord, thank you, thank you!" appeared on the screens as she led the singing. Most people were sitting, but about 10 women were standing swaying their bodies with arms extended skyward. When that song ended, Grady began his sermon. It was around noon.

His sermon that day was the sixth in a series focusing on Jesus' parables from the New Testament. He read from Matthew Chapter Seven describing the difference between a wise and foolish builder and spent a few minutes talking about the reading, making it relevant to his life and the lives' of others. The wise builder constructs his house on a rock, while the foolish one builds on sand. Be a wise builder by having "your foundation" in the Word and in the love of Jesus Christ, Grady said.

"You can have a good life without Christ; a good marriage and make a lot of money. You can be a little league baseball coach and even adopt a Third World baby, but sooner or later you'll need Jesus. The truth is that in this life there's going to be some rain, there's going to be some storms – the winds are going to blow. I admonish you today to check your foundation of God's Word or worldly standards."

Grady both in private counseling and his public preaching and teaching refers to his own background when for years his foundation was made of sand. Many times it seemed like quicksand. "I don't believe the Word of God because some preacher told me. I tried it my way, and it didn't work," Grady told his congregation. "God's way worked for me. I must bring my life in line with His Word."

He closed the service with a short Bible reading and a prayer. "Every head lowered, every eye closed," Grady said. "You might be like I was. I did some bad things but overall I was pretty good...God is bringing you back home today. Change your floor plan today." The service ended at 12:30 p.m., and Grady walked from the pulpit to the middle of the sanctuary where worshippers spoke to him as they left. Grady shook hands with some, hugged others and said, "God is good. God is a great God!"

* * *

Rev. Nadine Rountree, the church's worship leader, has been married to Keith Rountree for 19 years, and they have three children and live in McDonough, Georgia, a short drive north of Griffin. Keith is training to become a church deacon. During the service I attended, he operated the technology needed for the background music and for the screens behind the pulpit as his wife was singing. They met Grady in 2001 in Hampton, Georgia, through Zion Baptist. Like others, they followed him to New Mercy. Keith is a food inspector for the US Department of Agriculture, and his wife is a medical assistant for Kaiser Permanente. Both were reared in the Baptist faith, and both said they remembered the shouting and loud preaching of some ministers and the use of "fear." It's different at New Mercy, they said. "No one is worried about that (fear) here at New Mercy," Rev. Rountree said. "If I love you, I can look beyond your past, what you've done...Pastor Grady says, 'Whatever we do, do it in love.' It's a constant reminder we have to love each other."

I interviewed the couple after the church service at Grady's house. Keith agreed with his wife. "That's the message of Christ. It's love...The fear you're talking about is not God's Word. Jesus is all about Grace... There's no fear in love."

* * *

158

Years ago when Grady was a drug addict spending times behind bars, he said he thought of a title for a book about his life, *To Dance with the Devil's Daughter.* The "devil's daughter" is street-talk for cocaine, and he had allowed her to control his life for a long time. With God's help and Kathleen's love, he had finally whipped the devil's daughter. I asked Grady at his home after attending his service and with Kathleen preparing an afternoon meal, if he has long thoughts of regret. Do those years of drug addiction, incarceration, and neglect of family weigh heavy on his heart like an anvil on a bare foot? His answer surprised me. "I don't think about it," he said. "I'm under the blood, and my past has been forgiven. I don't deny my past, but I know it has been forgiven." He's under the blood of Christ, the World Redeemer.

I was surprised by another answer Grady gave me that day when I asked him about future plans for his church, his life. "I don't look that far ahead," he said. "He's running the show today; I'm not." *He* is God. The ministry will continue to be his life's work, but it's God who determines the details. "It's all in His hands, not mine."

FOURTEEN

Several years ago Ed Shepard had two dreams in which God instructed him to do something he at first would not accept. What God wanted defied Ed's upbringing, his values, and the way he viewed himself in the context of others. Refusing God's call can be difficult. Ed found that out. God wanted Ed to help poor African American children living in Griffin, Georgia. Shepard is a 66-year-old southern white man with, until he experienced those dreams, a lifetime of "prejudice" toward African Americans, he said. The dreams occurred on consecutive nights. The second and final dream led to Ed meeting Grady, a man who helped change Shepard's life. God was taking Ed in places he never would've dreamed.

During the first dream, Ed was in a basement made out of wood. The basement was old and needed painting. It appeared as a gloomy place, one of sadness. It was dim in the basement, almost dark, full of children, but he could not clearly see their faces, Ed said. "I couldn't tell whether they were black or white children," he said. "I did see some adults with the children. I remember that. The next day I couldn't get the dream out of my mind, and I talked to some of my pastor friends about it."

The dream bothered Ed the following day. That night something else happened that still amazes him. He had another dream almost identical to the one he had the night before. "During the second dream

I was in the basement again, but I could see better this time," he said. "It was full of children but this time I could see that 95 percent were black. I could see their faces." This dream bothered him more than the first one did. It more than bothered him; it tormented him. The problem was, Ed said, he knew what God wanted, and it caused him anxiety and "many sleepless nights." God was instructing Shepard to use his life to help poor African American children. A lifetime of prejudice is hard to overcome even when God is calling. Ed began to understand it all, God speaking to him through his dreams. There was resistance, though, for days. "I didn't want to respond to the second dream. God whipped me," Ed said. "God would not allow me to sleep. Finally, I fell to my knees at home and said, 'Okay, God, I'm yours." When he surrendered to God that day on his knees in tearful prayer in his house, Ed said he knew he had to act. He knew what he was going to do, and he saw clearly the path God had laid before him. Ed went to work. He contacted pastors he knew through his involvement in the Flint River Baptist Association. He sought Rev. Norm Daugherty who is now dead, but then was the pastor at New Salem Baptist Church in Griffin where Ed was a member. Ed also contacted Rev. Nathaniel Lee of Zion Baptist Church in Hampton and the same church where Grady was serving as assistant pastor. Ed arranged a meeting among himself, Daugherty and Lee. Ed knew exactly what he was going to propose: A summer vacation Bible school program for African American children in Griffin. God wanted that, and He wanted Ed to see it through.

This program came to be known as "Kid's Explosion" and was first organized about eight years ago. Until New Mercy opened, adults like Ed and others provided Bible study classes for the children in the public park and gymnasium. The program grew over the years until Ed and others who helped the program determined a church was needed in the children's neighborhood. Ed during this period had been introduced to Grady and had attended his Bible study classes. He was looking for an African American minister to pastor the new church. Ed wanted Grady for the assignment and pledged support from New Salem Baptist Church. More than just a working relationship developed between the two men.

"I have no friend better than Grady Caldwell. I've met many people, but God has tied us together," Ed said. "I wish I had words to explain that but I can't. He's the closest friend I have."

I asked Grady about his relationship with Ed Shepard.

"Only God could've knitted us together. We came from entirely different ends of the spectrum," Grady said. "Through this whole process we call each other 'twin brothers.' He's just a little taller and has more hair. And the thing about our friendship is that it's complete candor. We are totally honest with one another. I think the world of Ed Shepard."

Ed once served as an ordained deacon for Faith Baptist Church in Griffin but for the past 14 years has been a member of New Salem where there are about 300 members, including only "two or three" minority families. The church is predominately white and working class. New Mercy is mostly African American and poor. Since New Mercy opened in 2008, New Salem has given the church about $65,000 through monthly checks, Ed said. Because of the good work Grady and his church is doing and the fact that many members of New Mercy simply do not have the financial resources to support a church on their own, Ed was able to convince his church to help. Help must come from elsewhere. The dreams Ed had and the call from God have been answered. The giving will continue.

"We have them in our monthly budget. We've sent them monthly checks since their founding," Shepard said. "As long as I am finance chairman, we'll continue sending them money." Financial help for New Mercy has come from others sources as well.

Ed said he serves as chief financial officer for both New Salem and New Mercy, indicating the close relationship between the two churches. Grady is thankful for this, calling it "God's will" that these two churches have been able to work so well together over the past few years. "One reason they continue to give is that we have been good stewards of God's money," Grady said. "We can account for every penny that comes through here (New Mercy) from our partners."

I met Ed Shepard in July 2012 at McDonald's restaurant in Griffin as he was on his way to help Grady at Anne Street Elementary School where they had conducted the Kid's Explosion Vacation Bible School for the past three years. The night before we met more than 100 children had attended as Ed and several other adults provided instruction in the Word. Ed was tall and thick-shouldered with sturdy hands, and he had thick gray hair and wore glasses. He was wearing shorts and a Kid's Explosion gray T-shirt and hanging around his neck was a white nametag that read "Ed." He lived in Molena, a small town about a 35-minute drive from Griffin. We sat in a booth and talked about his life, the dreams he had, and his relationship with Grady. More than once he became visibly emotional. Those two dreams and meeting Grady has "changed my life," he said.

"My attitude has totally changed about people," he said, "whether they're African American, Chinese, Japanese, or whatever. I don't care anymore. My prejudices are gone. There's no prejudice left in me. They all need the love of Jesus Christ."

When a person bleeds, any person from anywhere, "the blood is all red," Ed said. All need to be reminded of the blood of Christ.

Ed and his wife Pauline have three children, and the couple has developed a "very close" relationship with Grady and Kathleen. They spend time together, and they pray together, laugh together, and talk about the changes in their lives. And together, Ed said, they are guided by God and doing His work. Both Ed and Grady have testimonies about love and forgiveness. On one of my visits to Grady's house, Kathleen served dinner and with it came home-grown tomatoes from Ed's garden in Molena. The tomatoes were plump, shiny red, and delicious. I grow tomatoes myself, and Ed's were as good as any I had ever had. It was a small gift from the Shepards to the Caldwells, an African American couple who has helped change Ed's life in unpredictable ways.

Ed was born in Norfolk, Virginia, in 1946, and said he grew up in a "good home" but not a Christian one. His father was a carpenter, and his mother worked inside the home caring for Ed and his two brothers. Sometimes, but not regularly, Ed did attend a Primitive Baptist Church when he was growing up. But Christianity had had little influence on his life until one night in 1967. His younger brother Graham died on that night in a fishing accident. Ed was both devastated and frightened. "That's when I got scared," he said. "I began to wonder, 'What's next? Where did he (Graham) go?' " While mourning his brother's death, Ed began to think hard for the first time about what is it that awaits us after death?

He was a troubled young man. He had been living in Jacksonville, North Carolina, when his brother died, and oddly on the same night a minister was making regular visits in Ed's neighborhood. The minister came to the Shepard's house. Ed spoke at length with him and the minister talked about death, heaven and hell, using specific Bible passages to console Ed. "For the first time in my life someone helped me understand the Bible," he said. "We talked about dying, and I accepted Jesus Christ as my Savior."

During this period Ed was a member of the North Carolina National Guard, and after Dr. Martin Luther King, Jr. was assassinated in 1968, his unit was sent to Wilmington, North Carolina, where civil unrest had occurred by African Americans outraged by the killing. The same was happening in many American cities. Ed's unit spent three weeks there under very dangerous conditions. "Boy, it was terrible at first. There was a lot of rioting, burning, and looting," he said. The anger and sadness felt by African Americans in Wilmington was the same as Grady Caldwell's own emotions that night in Albany, Georgia, after King was killed. Ed was not hurt during his duty in Wilmington. The first night there his unit was not given ammunition. By the second night their rifles were loaded. "I never shot at anyone. I only had to draw my weapon once," he said.

Ed worked for Cook's Discount and Department Store in North Carolina and by the early 1970s had been transferred to Griffin, Georgia. He joined the Georgia National Guard and eventually left Cook's to work for the United Parcel Service. He retired from UPS after 26 years. Growing up in the segregated South of the mid-20th century, Ed's attitudes and values were reflective of the white culture during this period. He had prejudicial views about African Americans. This was his birthright. God changed all of that. Today Ed devotes much of his time to New Salem Baptist Church, works in his garden, and thanks God for the dreams that changed his life and led him to Grady. "He's one of a kind. There's no other word for that man," Ed said. "His testimony is so strong. I guess I respect him as much as any man in the world."

Grady offered the same to Ed Shepard.

"Our friendship is genuine," Grady said. "I feel the same about him and respect him as much as any man I know."

* * *

Kid's Explosion, the Bible school program that began first in Ed's dream, met from July 9-12 in 2012 and set a record of "274 children on one night," Grady said. It was the eighth year for the program. Shepard attended every night, helping African American children from five to 18 years old. About 30 adults helped each night, from seven to nine, sharing Bible lessons, offering arts and crafts, and organizing skits for the older children. Vans and buses from New Mercy and other churches begin picking up children around six p.m. to bring them to Anne Street Elementary and take them home after the program ended.

"God was working through Ed to make Kid's Explosion possible. That's the only way to explain it," Grady said. "Ed and I had nothing to do with it. That was God's work."

Ed didn't know exactly where his dream would end. He said he finally put his trust in God, decided to help African American children, met Rev. Grady Caldwell, and helped him found New Mercy. That help continues today. Ed said his life now is one of a deeper humanity, a better understanding of God's purpose, and a better understanding of all people.

* * *

Douglas S. Hollberg was serving on the Griffin City Commission as mayor when Grady appeared several years ago before commissioners asking to rent the vacant building that now houses the New Mercy congregation. Hollberg was supportive and said, "I was attracted to Grady's vision of changing that neighborhood." The neighborhood near the church is often referred to as Spring Hill, and there has been, since the church opened, much "good work" occurring there through Grady's ministry. "It's a whole lot more stable over there now," Hollberg said. "You don't have so many kids just hanging out and gambling and breaking windows like they used to...Some places over there had been almost like a battle zone, but not anymore."

Hollberg was born in 1968 at Shaw Air Force Base in Sumter, South Carolina, and his family moved to Griffin a few years later. In 1990 he graduated from North Georgia Military College in Dahlonega and had sought to serve in the military but was given a medical discharge because of an eye disease, he said. He returned to Griffin and began working in the family's residential property business. He knows well the neighborhood around New Mercy. Several years ago he made a business decision to build affordable houses in that area, but the project stalled during the recent economic downturn. His efforts were aimed at trying to "clean up that neighborhood" and make it a better place to live.

"I wanted to change that area by building new homes," Hollberg said. "Grady's trying to do it with God, and you can actually see a change in that area through prayer and patience and faith in God."

Hollberg is one of about 1,000 members of First Baptist Church in Griffin, and his church was one of several that have helped New Mercy since its founding. First Baptist donated a van to New Mercy, and several of its members worked many hours to renovate the building. Hollberg himself has done other things to help. He has allowed New Mercy to occupy one of his apartments in that neighborhood, rent free, where a deacon in training currently lives. The deacon conducts regular Bible study classes, counsels those in need, and carries out New Mercy's ministry. The regular presence of those from the church willing to help has made the difference, Hollberg said. There's something else happening in Griffin because of Grady and his ministry.

"Different folks seem to gravitate toward Grady," Hollberg said. "Churches sometimes don't work well with one another, but Grady has been a bridge among the churches in Griffin. His vision has brought many people together."

EPILOGUE

Around 2000 when I was working on my first book that included Grady and Kathleen Caldwell, I interviewed her at her home in Albany. Grady was in prison at the time. I sensed then, after about an hour with her, she was a person of indomitable strength and beauty and love. Both family love and love for God. She was a woman of deep faith. After spending many hours with her and Grady for more than a year as we worked on this book together, I realized I was right. She had to possess these qualities to endure the ordeal to which her husband subjected her. She could've gone away. She could've divorced him, but she didn't. Her calling was greater, as she understood it. The story of Rev. Grady Caldwell is one of redemption, but it is also a love story.

Over the past eleven years or so, Grady Caldwell's life has been one of seeking restoration with his family and service to God and others. It took him years to get to such a place, but he has. His journey continues through God's love, and love from Kathleen, and their children and friends. He has surrendered himself to God. Grady makes no long-term plans for his ministry at New Mercy. That, he said, is what God does and he only makes himself available to listen to God. When the path is revealed, Grady follows. To non-believers that may seem suspect.

I know from where he has come, and I know the loving manner in which he leads his church. He was once a man self-absorbed through drugs, sex, and his own big ego. He was once a selfish man, and he was that way for many years. It took him years and years to purge those demons. Many times in his letters to Kathleen from prison he referred to "Satan's" grip over him. Satan now has been defeated. To watch him now, to hear him teach, and listen to those who admire him, those he has helped, the conclusion is easy. He exudes the love and compassion of Jesus Christ. The Bible is full of many stories. The most powerful ones to me are those about love, of finding yourself in the other, of curbing the human ego that resides in all of us. When that kind of love becomes recognizable, it represents one of the highest forms of humanity. I feel that today about Grady and Kathleen. I've seen it in action, and it is a beauty to behold.

Grady's own personal journey *had* to be about love, forgiveness, and redemption. Had he not chosen that route and continued the life of drugs and crime, he may have eventually killed his body and soul. Through God and those who loved him, he finally found the strength to recover, to love his family again properly, but not without suffering. The idea that suffering leads to spiritual growth is a powerful Christian theme that is evoked best by the image of Christ on the cross. Through suffering comes wisdom. Grady found that wisdom.

While Grady's story is rooted in his strong faith and in his love for Jesus Christ and His teachings, several times being with him, hearing him teach and pray with others, I realized the universal qualities of his life story. Not that most people spend years addicted to drugs and in prison, but regardless of one's religion, receiving acceptance and authentic love from others can be an intoxicating elixir. His life now is about demonstrating that kind of love for others, for those who are hurting, those who are lost and those coming to New Mercy for his guidance. This kind of love can be difficult to express. It often challenges our own prejudices as was the case with Grady himself who said before he attended the Graves Springs training camp for the Albany High football team in the 1960s, he did not trust white people. At camp and on that team he learned there were some "good white people," not all were bad. He began to change his thinking after that experience. Or it can be similar to what happened to Ed Shepard. For most of his life he was prejudiced toward African Americans. His heart changed after two dreams and a call from God that he answered: Acceptance then love.

Grady Caldwell changed other things about his life besides turning away from drugs and to God's will. For years he refused to recognize his first child, Yolanda, born out of wedlock, and she was not Kathleen's child. Although he and Kathleen were dating at the time, Grady had been with another girl. Finally, both Grady and Kathleen would accept and embrace Yolanda, asking for her forgiveness, and including her as part of their family. Yolanda was at their home Father's Day June 2012. She was part of the laughter and love I felt in that house that day.

There were many profound stories I learned while working on this book, including those from Yolanda and Grady and Kathleen's other three children. I'm grateful for their candor, and I admire their strength, their willingness to forgive, and their own personal accomplishments. It would not have been unexpected, as I conducted interviews with them, to learn that because their father had caused them much embarrassment and pain they had turned away from him. This was not the case. Once Grady finally quit taking drugs, he was able to love properly again and they were able to forgive him and return his love. Pain still lingers. Rev.

Carmen Caldwell said she continues to seek counseling partly because of the years of loss and disappointment from an absentee and drug-addicted father, a father whom she loved and admired when she was a little girl. Full restoration and reconciliation can sometimes take a lifetime.

Years of heavy drug use did other things to Grady besides the pain he caused to those who loved him. His memory of past events is often unclear, not about everything but some things. He attributes this to the drugs. Several times during our interviews I'd ask him a question about a person or event from his past, and he would hesitate a few seconds and say, "Bill, you'll have to ask Kat about that. I just don't remember exactly. Those drugs messed my mind up. I don't always remember everything." When this occurred, I would confer with Kathleen, and she would always help me find the answer I was searching for. He was always honest. At times painfully honest.

Like all great teachers, Grady teaches by example. He does not attempt to cajole or threaten someone with going to hell in order to make a point. He's not loud when he preaches. He doesn't use fear or intimidation. He will always use his own powerful testimony, his own discovery about God's love, and the availability of redemption regardless of how far someone has fallen. He fell a long way himself and came back again. Through God's love, he said, all people can rise again, learn to love again and care for others. This is Grady's lesson for everyone. He uses his own past as a guide to compassion and to putting oneself in the eyes of another. Grady said it's what Jesus calls everyone to do.

When the idea of a new church was being discussed and offered to Grady, he would eventually name it by referring to the Old Testament. He went to Lamentations Chapter Three: 22-23: "It is of the Lord's mercies that we are not consumed, because His compassions fail not. They are new every morning."

Senior Pastor Grady Lee Caldwell, Jr. was saved by a merciful God and his wife Kathleen whose love was everlasting. Now the two of them, along with Rev. Carmen Caldwell, have built and continue to build a church of love and mercy. They have touched the hearts of many. Their work goes on with God's guidance.

In front of New Mercy is a large white sign indicating the name of the church and its senior pastor. At the bottom of the sign is God's message from Lamentations. "His Mercies Are New Every Morning." The senior pastor at New Mercy was once the young boy who knew Dr. Martin Luther King, Jr., was mentored by civil rights leaders in Albany, Georgia, made his own contributions to civil rights history while becoming a young man of much promise and potential. Then he fell into a hellish pit of drug addiction and crime for nearly 20 years. He rose from it all with the help of God and his family, and he has created a loving ministry in Griffin, Georgia, for people in need of healing.

Truly, His mercies are new every morning.

ACKNOWLEDGEMENT

Thanks to Grady, Kathleen, their children and all of their family members and friends who spoke to me about Grady's life as I was working on this book. Working with Grady and learning about his redemptive life has enriched my own life. I felt very fortunate all along the way to bring his story to a world of readers.

The Grady and Kathleen Caldwell story is illustrative of what love and faith in God can overcome.

Thanks to my wife Phyllis who helped with ideas, editing, and the support I needed to finish the book. She sees things that I can't. I needed her constant encouragement – and always will.

Bill Lightle
Fayetteville, Georgia
December 2012

Bill Lightle has been honored by a Georgia State Senate Resolution for "his passion for education, history and the furtherance of social justice." He is the author of *Made or Broken: Football & Survival in the Georgia Woods; Mill Daddy: The Life & Times of Roy Davis;* and *My Mother's Dream: Baseball with the Bankers.* He lives in Fayetteville, Georgia, with his wife, Phyllis, and teaches at Fayette County High School.

PICTURES

Grady Caldwell is on the second row second from left. This was taken sometime in the 1950s at Albany State College. Grady's mother, Leola, had enrolled him in an educational enrichment program.

Grady graduated from Albany High School in 1967. He was the first African American to play on the school's football team.

Kathleen Jones Caldwell graduated from Albany High in 1968. She begun dating Grady while the two were students there. Both endured acts of racism at the school.

Grady ran unsuccessfully for the Albany City Commission in the 1970s. By this period he was becoming a local political leader.

The Caldwell family in 1986, before Grady's fall into drug addiction. Back row is Daphne and on the front row Carmen, Lee, Kathleen and Grady.

Grady and his mother, Leola, at an Albany restaurant. They were celebrating her 98th birthday in 2007. She was a teacher who always stressed to her children the importance of an education.

Dr. William Anderson and his son Dr. Gil Anderson taken in 2012. William Anderson was a surrogate father to Grady and president of the Albany Movement, the key civil rights group in Albany in the 1960s. Gil and Grady were close friends. Grady met Dr. Martin Luther King, Jr. at the Anderson home.

Grady and Kathleen traveled to Israel in 2009 with a church group.
This was taken near Jerusalem.

These are some of the current church leaders at New Mercy Baptist
Church in Griffin, Georgia, where Grady is senior pastor:
First row left to right are Rev. Nadine Rountree, Rev. Ann Sutton, and
Sister Hyson Driver-Tucker. Back row left to right are Deacon Arthur
Atkins, Deacon Reginald Keith Rountree, Deacon Paul Sutton, and
Deacon Marcellus Blalock.

Loretta Joyce Travers, Grady's sister and only sibling. With her sons, left to right, Malcolm and Theo Travers.

Dr. James and Ella Woods of Albany, Georgia, are close friends of the Caldwells. The Woods often prayed with and provided support for Kathleen during Grady's long period of drug addiction.

Ed and Pauline Shepard became friends with Grady and Kathleen after Grady became pastor at New Mercy. This was taken in the Shepard home in Molena, Georgia, in 2012. Shepard's church, New Salem Baptist in Griffin, became a partner church to New Mercy. Shepard said his friendship with Grady has "changed my life" helping him overcome his longstanding prejudice toward minorities.

Daniel Simmons is senior pastor at Mount Zion Baptist Church in Albany. Here he is attending Kathleen's retirement reception in 2006 after her long career working for Albany State University.

*Taken at the Caldwell home outside of Griffin in 2012 in celebration
of Kathleen's and Carmen's birthdays. Kathleen is sitting. Left to right:
Ernesto and his wife, Daphne Caldwell Rackley; Carmen Caldwell;
Grady; Grady's daughter Yolanda Graham; Ronda and Lee Caldwell.*

*The grandchildren of Kathleen and Grady Caldwell from left to right:
Grayson Lawrence Caldwell, Grayson Elias Graham,
Asia Simone Rackley, and Sydney Rackley.*

182

In the middle is Kathleen's mother, Lois Jones. She was 91 in 2010 at an Atlanta hospital. Kathleen and Grady are in the background and joined by members of both families. Lois taught Kathleen and her other children to stand "strong" against racism as they were growing up in the 1950s and '60s.

Kathleen and Grady in 2012. Now a marriage of love and faith that endured years of pain caused by Grady's drug addiction.

Grady Caldwell, senior pastor of New Mercy Baptist Church in Griffin, Georgia.

CPSIA information can be obtained at www.ICGtesting.com
Printed in the USA
LVOW12s1105220713

344003LV00001B/5/P